Still Walking

The Story of a Life Full of Love, Laughter and Lessons

Rob Oliver

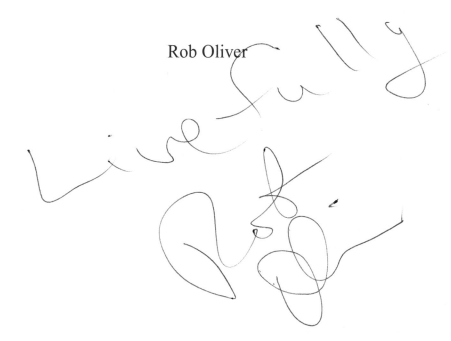

Still Walking
Copyright © 2010 by Rob Oliver

ISBN (978-0-578-07384-2)

Dedication

To Josh, Lauren, Chloe
and Becky

for keeping my heart and
life filled to the brim.

Table of Contents

Table of Contents

Prologue

Time slows down to an absolute standstill. I'm supposed to be asleep. I want to be asleep. I need to be asleep. But I'm not asleep. For some reason, I just can't get there. All I can do right now is lie here and think. It has been one of those weeks. Nothing seems to have gone right. Work has been rough. My wife, Becky, is mad at me. I have a couple of health issues and my attempt to do something helpful at church backfired as someone was upset by it. Now, I just lie in bed. I can't get up. I don't want to wake Becky up. I can't turn the TV on. I just lie here. It's times like these when my mind starts to run wild. These are the nights when my thoughts are full of "what if" and "if only" and "I wish I could". My marriage, like every marriage, has its issues. Part of being husband and wife is bringing your different personalities together to form a relationship. That part is hard enough even without adding in a disability. Now there's a major complicating factor.

Work is enjoyable, but it does keep me busy. Some days I wish I could get more done. There's a certain amount of frustration in that the only place I can find a job is working with people with disabilities. I have training, education and intelligence to contribute to society at large. Having a disability shouldn't mean that I can only work in the disability field.

When it comes to helping other people, it really stinks when you try to do the right thing and it is not appreciated. Or if you try to do the right thing and you are thoroughly criticized for it. Those are the experiences that make you wonder if you should just stop. It might be nice for the people that criticize to be the ones doing the work. As I think about it, it would be fun to let them do something and then criticize them for how they do it.

Like I said, my mind is a jumble of thoughts as I lie here. The longer I think about it though, the more I realize that my attitude is way out of line. The nice thing about being awake in the middle of the night is that there are no distractions. I have some time to talk to God about what is happening. It's amazing that when I'm talking to God about what I want to change in other people, He takes the opportunity to show me what needs to be changed in me. Tonight, as I am thinking about the difficult circumstances that I'm facing, my mind starts to reflect on how I actually got here.

I start to think about my life experiences. What has happened to bring me to where I am today? What lessons have I learned so far? What really is important about life? The more I think about it, the more stories, lessons and experiences come into my mind. It doesn't take too long before I smile. Then I realize that it's the middle of the night, it's dark, I'm by myself and I'm smiling.

My life experiences have taught me so much. They make me smile. They make me laugh. Some of them make me cry. I wonder to myself if anyone else can benefit from the lessons I've learned, so I determine to write them down. Maybe there's something in this book that you can learn from. Maybe you will be amused by it. Maybe this will be an opportunity for you to be reassured that everyone has problems. I'm not sure what this book will mean to you, but I hope that it will be an inspiration.

2

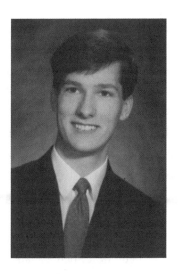

Chapter One
Baby Steps

I've come to understand that my lifelong plague of being late for everything started as an infant. My poor mother had to wait more than a week after her expected due date for me to arrive. To further complicate matters, it took 24 hours worth of labor to bring me into the world. Finally, there I was. I was breathing my first breath and experiencing the first moments of the roller coaster called life.

Because this book is written from my perspective, I'm going by what I've been told since I don't have a whole lot of recollections about those early years. I know that sometime during the first year of my life, my parents opened their home to a quiet and reserved young man by the name of John Nobles. He became my big brother. John had been through some foster care homes. He soon became an integral part of our family. As I grew into a toddler, John became my babysitter, mentor, wrestling coach, playmate and overall hero.

John's entire family had come through the foster care system. After being separated from his siblings at a fairly young age, he clung to his new family. My sister, born shortly after I turned two, seemed to fill a sister-shaped hole in John's life. John's shyness seemed to slip away for a moment as he ran from door to door telling everyone, "It's a girl!" Somehow this enthusiasm was conveyed to me and had a lasting impact. Instead of viewing my younger sister as an irritant or rival, I saw this little girl as someone to be loved and protected.

Some people have been described as "an accident waiting to happen". I think a more accurate description of me was "an accident in progress". As I grew up, it seemed that I was often spraining an ankle, falling down and scraping an elbow or a knee or even getting stung by a jellyfish. At the age of five, I had my first major injury. On the outside of our church building was a concrete stairwell that led to a basement door. It was approximately 8 feet deep with a railing around the top of it that would prevent someone from accidentally falling in. After the service was done we boys would run outside and sit on that railing. Sometimes, we would spin around on it. One night while I was hanging on the bar, my hands slipped and I lost my grip on the railing. I plummeted to the bottom of the stairwell, rubbed a few layers of skin off my face and arms and knocked myself out as I landed on my head.

The Bryn Mawr Hospital was only a few blocks away and I was rushed there immediately. I was diagnosed with a concussion (my first of multiple) and kept in overnight for observation. Lindsay Parks, a family friend and practicing doctor at the hospital, came in to visit me through the night just to check on me. As much as I could understand at the age of five, I was very glad to have someone who I knew as a friend helping to take care of me.

My face was pretty banged up and I had a variety of bumps and bruises on my head and body. The doctors suggested that I stay home from school for a few days to recover. This would be my first of many "mini-vacations" from school because of injury or illness.

From the time that we were little, I remember playing and talking with my younger sister Rebekah. I'm fairly certain that there were times I did not treat her nicely, but for the most part we got along very well. As kids we rode our bikes together to and from elementary school. It was during a morning ride to school that a problem became evident. We would ride down the hill from our house to a bus route which had a slight uphill grade the entire way to school. As we pedaled up the slight incline my legs would get so tired that I actually had to stop. As I sat waiting for a few minutes to rebuild my strength, Rebekah would ride her bike around me in circles. Before long, I would feel strong enough and then pedal the rest of the way to school.

The weakness began to affect other areas of my life. There was a convenience store just down the road from our house. Mom would send me down to get a gallon of milk a few times a week. On more than one occasion, my hands would give out as I was trying to carry the milk home. Mom and Dad were concerned about this and took me to a variety of doctors. Children's Hospital of Philadelphia administered a variety of tests to see if they could pinpoint the problem.

As a six or seven year old kid, I did not understand all of the tests. They tested my brain activity by attaching a number of leads and wires to my head. My mother is a bit of a neat freak and had impressed on me the necessity of cleanliness. Imagine my consternation when they took paste and rubbed it in my hair to make the leads stick. Washing my hair afterwards was a complete and utter disaster. Every time we washed it, huge chunks of paste came out. We had to wash my hair four times before it would pass for clean.

The battery of tests to which I was submitted was very extensive. In addition to CAT scans and x-rays, there were a variety of blood tests. A doctor in a white coat took me into the exam room and told me that they needed to draw blood for five or six different tests. He said that in order to make sure they did not have to poke me with more than one needle, he was going to use a butterfly needle that fed into a three-way valve. His plan was to put a vial on each valve and draw blood as quickly as possible. The difficulty was that he could not get a vacuum to form at the valves and instead of it drawing the blood out, the blood would leak from the other two valves before he could get each vial attached. Before long there was a puddle of blood on the side of the examination table and it started to drip onto the floor. He finally figured out the system, got the vials filled and sent them off to the lab. I'm not sure why, but I was not afraid during this process. It actually served to make me comfortable with having blood drawn, which became a very useful coping mechanism in later years.

Mom came down to visit me every day, for which I was very thankful. It was a weird situation because I wasn't actually sick. I was just having a bunch of tests done. My roommates were all sick. The girl in the bed across from me had just had major brain surgery. Half of her head was shaved and there was a large and nasty looking scar that formed a semicircle on the side of her head. There was a toddler in the bed next to me that had fallen out of a third story window and was injured severely. I wasn't feeling bad at all, so it was an opportunity for me to have some new experiences. There were arts and crafts activities every day, an unlimited supply of popsicles, a toy room to play in, kids to play with, and no school! Thankfully, there was a McDonald's in the lobby and sometimes, when my family came to visit, we would go down there to eat. It was very helpful in making the experience seem less institutional. Looking back on it, it is ironic that a McDonald's would be the one place I felt "the comforts of home".

My parents met with the doctors after the test results had been analyzed. The doctors determined that I had a mild, but progressive, form of muscular dystrophy. They told my parents to be prepared for continuing weakness that would lead to paralysis. The doctors explained that it was very likely that I would be in a wheelchair by the time I reached my 30s. My parents never told me the diagnosis. Thankfully, as I grew older it became increasingly obvious that this diagnosis was incorrect. Instead of becoming weaker and weaker, my strength was growing and I was soon running and active, easily able to keep up with the other children.

I'm not saying that I became a tremendous athlete—far from it. Let's just say I was a late bloomer. Throughout my elementary school years, I was that kid picked last. When the teams were organizing , it wasn't a matter of who got me on their team—it was who had to have me.

The fact that I can remember the very first time that I caught a pop fly in kickball should give you an indication of my lack of athletic ability. I remember watching the ball go up and up, realizing that it was going to come to me. Jeff, the kid that had kicked it, hollered that I was not going to catch it. I looked at the ball, got my arms ready to catch it and then it hit me. My arms were stinging, but I held on as tight as I could. I was waiting for the ball to bounce off my chest and out of my arms, but it did not. It took me a split second before I realized that I had actually caught it! I didn't drop it! Unfortunately, the joy that I had was completely my own. My classmates were all of the opinion that I should have caught it. When I told this story at the dinner table, Mom and Dad told me that I did good. Did "good"? That was all? I thought it was awesome! Looking back on it, I realize that it wasn't really something to get excited about. However, it was the first time that I really felt like I was contributing to the team. Instead of being put in a spot where I was the least detrimental, I was now an asset.

From there, things moved pretty quickly and I soon caught up to the rest of my classmates in athletic ability. As a result of my childhood weakness, I was never very confident in my own abilities. Instead of taking the game-winning shot, I was much happier to pass to the guy who would make the shot. It's odd how valuable lessons can be learned at a young age and yet forgotten so quickly. We all need to be reminded that sometimes it's okay to take a step back and let somebody else shine. Even more, it's okay to do what it takes to help somebody else shine.

Chapter Two
He Leadeth Me

My dad, David, was a math teacher, but spent his summers preaching. Shortly after my sister was born, he left his teaching career to become a full-time preacher. My mother, Melody, was extremely supportive of him. He did a lot of traveling, yet somehow she always managed to include him in our lives. It didn't matter if I was doing well in school or struggling, he had the inside scoop. Often, he would be gone for a month or two at a time. During those times, I would talk to him on the phone and he always knew what we needed to talk about. Mom did a pretty amazing job with that.

The really cool part about having a preacher for a dad was the summers. He had a gospel tent that he took with him to a few different places each summer. Since we were off school, the entire family traveled together. One of the places that he loved to go was Matoaca, Virginia. We were there for at least one month every summer of my youth.

Putting the tent up and taking it down were exciting experiences! My dad is a bit of a perfectionist (okay, he's a lot of a perfectionist.) Everything needed to be done a certain way, but he still managed to find odd jobs for me to help with.

I managed to enjoy myself quite nicely in the time between pitching the tent and taking it down. There was usually time for some children's meetings in the morning, but in the afternoons, I had a lot of free time. The campground that we stayed at had a pool and a lake. Most of the time, you would find me either swimming or fishing. Each summer a group of six or eight guys in their late teens and early twenties came with us to help my dad. They were great manual laborers in putting up the tent, and they also helped out with children's meetings.

Those meetings were really valuable experiences for me. I learned a lot of Bible stories, I learned how to talk to kids and those guys became my heroes.

When it was too cold to use the tent, Dad preached inside. There were times when he stayed at home and preached in the local area. Oftentimes, he would take me with him. When I was 10 years old, he was preaching at home, in Bryn Mawr. Mr. Bentley, a missionary from Malaysia, was there to help.

As I sat listening to the preaching one evening, I understood something that had never occurred to me before. Even though I was better behaved than many of my classmates and had heard more preaching than just about anyone else my age, I still did not have a personal relationship with God. The fact that I was "not that bad" and that I knew a lot about the Bible did not make me any closer to God than anyone around me. What prevented my

10

own relationship with God was the same thing that prevented everyone else's relationship with God. At only 10 years old I was already skilled at disobedience and dishonesty. On top of that, my heart was very capable of hate and nastiness that I could not help but express in the things I said. Those were the things that needed to be taken away for me to have any relationship with God. All my life I had known the story about Christ on the cross. I knew all the facts about how long it was dark, who else was crucified with him, what they accused him of, and the schedule of what happened. But it was on that night that I understood exactly what happened there. What happened there was for me. He was suffering for the things that I had done. My personal relationship with God started that night based solely on the fact that the Lord Jesus Christ gave His life so that I could be forgiven.

As I grew up, I began to wonder what God had planned for my life. I prayed about that and didn't really have any answers. I knew God had a plan for me, but I wasn't sure what it was. I wondered if God had a girl in mind for me. The one thing I was certain about was that whatever God's plan was, it was going to be good.

When I was around 15 years old, I read a book by Leighton Ford entitled "Sandy: A Heart for God". Dr. Ford tells the story of his oldest son, Sandy, a promising young man with a desire to serve God. The problem was that Sandy had a bad heart. At the age of 21, Sandy had open heart surgery to correct the problem. He passed away on the operating table.

There was a point in time where Sandy was in a wheelchair because of his physical condition. The way he lived his life in that chair showed the people around him just who he was. God

11

was able to use Sandy wherever he was and whatever his circumstances. In my struggles with understanding God's plan for my life, I remember praying that God would use me. I told God, "I want to be useful, whatever it takes, even if it's being in a wheelchair."

When I look back at that, I realize that God had a very special plan for me. I also realize that you should never offer to do something for God that you're not ready to do. I don't think that God put me in a wheelchair because of my prayer; I believe that God was getting me ready for His plan. It wasn't until a few months after my injury that I remembered this prayer, but it served as a comfort to know that God was in control and had a purpose for me.

Chapter Three
Becky

I attended many Bible conferences throughout my youth, and as a result developed friendships with people from around the country. One of those relationships was with Becky Clark, who lived near Pittsburgh. I met her when I was five years old and we got along very well. From then on, we saw each other a few times a year. When we were teenagers, she and one of her friends talked to me about their problems with guys. They would ask questions like, "Are there any good guys out there anymore?" Somehow I was too polite (or scared) to point out the fact that I was nice, considerate, unattached and apparently a friend in whom they could confide. I guess I didn't want to risk our friendship. We would talk by phone every few months, occasionally hang out and I did not want to mess that up.

13

I remember one time when I was visiting Becky's family, her mom and I were talking about who was dating who. She asked me if I was dating anybody and I told her I wasn't. She asked if I was interested in anyone. I mentioned a few names, but said that I was not sure about any of them. It was then that she confronted me with a question, "Have you thought about asking my daughter out?"

I'm not sure exactly what the expression was on my face, but I'm pretty sure that my cheeks turned bright red. I explained to her that I operated on an open door policy. Unfortunately, Becky always seemed to have someone else and that pretty much meant the door was closed. Thankfully, she accepted my explanation and the conversation moved on to another topic.

A few months later we were having a Bible conference at Bryn Mawr. A number of young people came and stayed at our house, including Becky and her boyfriend. I viewed Becky as a good friend, and I clearly remember observing their relationship during that stay. Her boyfriend was a funny guy. At one point he told a joke at her expense and then gave her a soft punch in the arm. I remember the hair on the back of my neck standing up. First, I would never put my girlfriend down publicly. Second, I would never lift a hand against her—even in jest.

A few months later, I got a call from Becky. When I asked her how she was doing, she said that she was going through a tough time. She and her boyfriend had just broken up. We talked about that for a little bit and then she told me that the reason she was calling was to invite me and my friends to a New Year's Eve party at her parents' house. Unfortunately for me, what I heard and what she said were two different things. My selective hearing as a male heard only that she broke up with her

14

boyfriend and wanted me to come out to visit her. I took it as a compliment and told her that I would be glad to come.

The joys of college break meant that I was able to plan for a few days at Becky's. We had a very nice time, talking, laughing, and watching movies. Then the trip hit a major snag. We were sitting in the family room, talking about life and other odds and ends. My mind went back to the open door policy conversation that I had with Becky's mom a few years before and I began to think that this might just be the open door. After hemming and hawing for a few minutes, I finally gathered up the courage to ask her out. Everything was deathly quiet for a few minutes while she just looked at me.

My heart sank when she refused. She told me that she was just coming out of a relationship and wanted to get her feet planted before she jumped into another one. The more she talked, the dumber I felt. I listened long enough to hear that the answer was "Not now." I went home the next day with questions in my head about the open door policy. Apparently, just because the door is open doesn't mean you have to walk through.

Over the next few months, Becky and I were in touch by phone. Our conversations were friendly, but very carefully skirted the issue of relationships. In February of 1993 we both attended a Bible study in Akron, Ohio. Becky was going to stay at her friend Debby's house with a large group of other young people. She invited me to come and stay there with them. I was in a bit of a quandary because my parents had friends in Akron with whom we always stayed. They had two children who were slightly younger than me and I tried to reach out to them. As their kids grew older, it became increasingly important to maintain positive friendships with them. A large part of me wanted to go where the young people were (and where Becky was) but another part of me understood that I had an opportunity to help a couple of kids. After a great deal of mental struggle, I told her that I thought it best for me to stay with my family.

When I did get to the conference, I was very happy to see her. We sat together at every session and ate our meals together. By Saturday afternoon, there was a buzz at the conference about Sunday's weather forecast. We were supposed to get a major snowstorm overnight that was going to continue through the day on Sunday. Although this was not a big issue to me, my friends, Allison and Michelle who lived near me in the Philadelphia area, were afraid to drive home in the snow. They decided that they had to leave early on Sunday to make sure they got home safely. After talking with them and hearing their concerns, I offered to drive for them so that they would feel safe. They said that would be wonderful and we left right after lunch on Sunday.

What I didn't realize was that Becky was very upset with me. Here was the man that was supposed to be interested in her and yet he would not stay where she was staying. Furthermore, he left the conference early with two other girls. She could not understand what was going on in my head at all!

Later in the week I called her and we talked. She had finally come to an understanding of my behavior the previous weekend. She understood that my reasoning was not a matter of what was most convenient to me, but what was best for others. During that conversation Becky told me that she'd been thinking about our relationship. While she felt the timing wasn't right for us to start a relationship at the beginning of January, she was wondering, "How about now?" That worked for me! It was a lesson learned; doing what is right is more than its own reward.

Chapter Four
A Bump in the Road

From my childhood I had two best friends, Mark Taylor and David Stewart. As we grew into teenagers, David's parents went out of their way to provide us with a safe place to hang out. Their continuing care earned them the nicknames of "Mom" and "Dad". In addition to opening their home, Mom and Dad Stewart were kind enough to invite us kids to participate each year in their summer vacation. They had a time-share on the Outer Banks of North Carolina in a little place called Duck. In the summer of 1993, a large group of us went down together.

Our usual rental was from Saturday to Saturday. Part of the traditional experience was to leave as early as possible on Saturday morning to ensure that we would arrive at the condo as soon as it was available. The trip took about eight hours so we were usually on the road by 5:30 a.m. That year Becky and I traveled together and caravanned with Mark who was driving his mom's van with Brian Parks and David. I had purchased a pair of CBs specifically for this trip and we enjoyed friendly banter the entire way. It made it very easy to know who had to stop and when. On top of that, Becky had to endure us being men, stopping to eat every time we were hungry.

As soon as we arrived and unpacked, we were able to hit the pool for a little while before settling in for the night. Becky and I had decided to go up to Matoaca, Virginia on Sunday morning to worship with the Christians there and visit John and Maggie Nobles and their family. In order to be on time we had to start out again at 6:00 a.m. Doing so on consecutive mornings was not enjoyable, but we felt it was important.

As always, it was wonderful to visit with the people in Matoaca. They had become almost like a second family to me. Every time I visited they made it obvious that they loved me. It was a joy to worship the Lord together and I shared some thoughts with them about how God was working. I used the example of Elijah who had prayed for rain and was looking for the clouds to come. His servant kept looking for something in the sky but didn't see anything until he finally saw a cloud the size of a man's hand. It was only a little cloud, but Elijah took it as God's answer and knew that the rain was coming. I was thinking that God sometimes shows us little things in life that are reminders of the fact that He is at work and has huge blessings in store for us.

One of the outstanding things during the first few days of our vacation was the strength of the surf. On the Outer Banks, they use red flags to tell you that the surf is too rough to go into the water. We had been there before when the surf was rough, but

18

this year was the roughest we had seen. In fact, on Tuesday a storm went by offshore. It churned up the surf so violently that when we went down to the beach in the morning, there was a line in the sand where the beach had been eaten away overnight. The line was just about where high tide was and the sand just dropped off 18 inches at that point. I was very impressed with the power of the water, but thought of it in terms of what it would do to nature, not what it would do to a person.

Every day had a certain routine to it. Responsibilities were passed around so that everybody had something to do at every meal. Mom Stewart did most of the meal preparation, but there were still the responsibilities of setting the table, cleaning the table, and doing dishes among other things. After breakfast, we had a brief time of devotions and then it was off to the beach. Certain traditions were carryovers from previous years. Someone would give thanks before every meal, but before that, a few of us guys had a traditional routine of phrases that had to be followed. One would say, "Rub a dub dub, thanks for the grub." Another would follow with, "Hey diddle diddle, thanks for the vittles." Followed by a chorus of, "Oh Lord we beseech Thee! Amen!" Quickly someone else would say, "Pass the gravy." Brian would end the whole thing by saying, "The best part about it is . . . it never gets old." Obviously, maturity was not one of our strong suits.

The rest of our typical days were spent on the beach where the girls spent the time soaking up the rays and the guys were busy playing some type of beach or water sport. On the days when the red flags were up, we spent a lot of time playing beach volleyball, miniature lacrosse and Frisbee. When there were no red flags, it was wave jumping, boogie boarding and body surfing. Body surfing was my water sport of choice and the Outer Banks was known to have the best surf on the East Coast.

One of the most enjoyable parts of the Outer Banks was that it was not very built up. There were not a lot of businesses or entertainment complexes. As young people, we took full advantage of the opportunity to create our own entertainment. After days filled with activities on the beach, we would head out after dinner to one of the local attractions such as the real grass miniature golf courses, the Dunes at Kill Devil Hills or the local shopping complex that had a T-shirt shop and ice cream store. The T-shirt shop there printed customized T-shirts. Somehow, it seemed like we talked about getting a commemorative T-shirt every year and yet I rarely came home with one.

We would usually return from our evening excursions after dark and a bunch of us kids would go for a walk on the beach. Most of the time there were bonfires around and we would either make our own or join someone else's. Sometimes we would sing and other times we would tell stories. Most of the stories that we told were about previous Outer Banks vacations. One of our favorites was the story about when Brian went crab fishing. Mike Kramer had brought down a number of crab reels. The crab reel is basically a spool of fishing line with a crank on it. You tie a piece of bait to the line, toss it in and when a crab grabs the bait, you just reel in the line. Mike gave Brian the reel that his grandfather had given him. It was old and well used and to Mike, it was a family heirloom. Brian had never used one before and he asked Mike, "Hey, how do you use this thing?" Mike told him to let out a little bit of line and toss the bait. Brian wound up, and to the dismay of everybody, tossed the bait, line and reel out into the water, never to be seen again.

Unfortunately, everybody found this story to be humorous except Mike.

After the bonfires, Becky and I would often go for a walk on the beach. We would sit on a blanket, look at the stars, watch the waves sparkle in the moonlight and talk. The fact that I was used to working the midnight shift at UPS began to have a detrimental effect on us. I was used to getting up in the morning around 10:30 or 11:00. Now that we were on vacation, I was waking up closer to 7:30 or 8:00 a.m. This change in schedule meant that I was exhausted by nightfall. More often than not, I would fall asleep right in the middle of our conversations. I'm not sure why Becky was so patient with me, but she let me sleep for an hour or so and when I woke up, we would head back to the condo. The Stewarts and my parents decided that it was not good for couples to be out on the beach at all hours of the night. They decided to impose a midnight curfew on everybody. I realize that they were trying to protect our relationships, however, the reality is that you don't need much protection from a snoring boyfriend.

On Friday, the last day of our beach time, the red flags were finally taken down. The surf was very good and the guys and I headed out into the waves. The waves were breaking fairly far out which meant that the ride to shore was a long and enjoyable one. Additionally, the speed of the waves made it an exhilarating rush. For those not familiar with body surfing, it relies on the same principles as regular surfing, however instead of standing on a board, your body is the board. No surfboards, no boogie boards, just you and the waves. We would swim out to the point just beyond where the waves were breaking and tread water, waiting for the next big wave to come. As we would see one rising just beyond us, one or two of us would swim towards the shore. The goal was for the wave to catch up to us just as it broke. The strength of the rolling wave would push us all the way to shore.

Some of the girls joined us, but after a few minutes decided that the waves were still a little bit too rough for them. In the meantime, I was truly enjoying some of the best body surfing that we had done in quite some time. The rides were fast and long and it was just a blast to swim back out and get ready for the next ride. As I was waiting, I saw a very nice wave approaching. I began to swim towards the shore and the wave crested just as it came to where I was. I was immediately propelled towards the shore, riding the wave to perfection. As I went farther in, I began to feel a little uncomfortable. I was no longer riding at the bottom of the wave where I was accustomed to being—I was a little bit higher in the wave. Before I knew what happened, the force of the wave was no longer driving me towards the shore but instead drove my head down towards the bottom where it smashed into the hard sand.

I immediately felt a pop in my neck and coldness throughout my body. I could not move anything at all. As the waves rolled above me I could do nothing but hold my breath, close my eyes and pray. The seconds seemed to pass by as hours. I called to God for help and received a peace that everything was going to be OK, no matter what happened. If I made it out of the water, I had the full confidence that He would be with me every step of the way. If I did not make it out, I had the full confidence that I knew where I was going and would see Him there. After what seemed like an eternity, my face cleared the water for a split second. I quickly gasped another breath into my burning lungs and waited. I wasn't sure what I was waiting for, but it was the only thing I could do, wait and pray.

It only took a few seconds before I felt strong arms grabbing under my shoulders and lifting my head out the water. My friend, Ken, had been in the water near where I was and saw my face when it cleared the water. When I did not stand up, he immediately realized that something was wrong. He started to look for me in the water. Thankfully, this was the early 90s and it was acceptable to wear brightly colored clothing. I had on a pair of purple swim trunks with yellow and pink trim. Those were the colors that he saw and reached for to save my life.

Ken grabbed me underneath my arms and supported my head on his chest. The waves kept coming in as he pulled me from the water. He worked to keep my head above the water, but occasionally the waves would roll over my face. As I saw them coming, I closed my eyes and held my breath. Ken called for help and a few more of the guys came over to get me out of the water completely.

As soon as they moved me away from the water, I told them that something was wrong with my neck. Immediately, the lifeguard came over and told them that my neck needed to be stabilized. They carefully picked my head and shoulders up off the sand to slide a boogie board underneath me. Someone held my head still to keep my neck from moving. It just so happened that one of the other people on the beach was a nurse. She began to ask me all kinds of questions about what I could feel and what was hurting me. After assessing my physical situation, she just kept talking to me. She spoke in a calming voice and kept up a conversation until the ambulance and paramedics arrived.

The paramedics handled me with great care. They immediately put a cervical collar around my neck to stabilize it as much as possible. With that done, they moved me onto a stretcher to take me to the ambulance. The difficulty was that we were on the beach and there was no way to roll the stretcher. Instead, my friends had to assist the paramedics in picking up the stretcher and carrying it across the hot sand, and finally, up the steps across the wooden bridge to get to the ambulance. I could see a look of discomfort on a few of their faces, but no one complained or missed a step the entire way.

Becky followed beside the stretcher as they walked down the beach, and joined me in the ambulance as they prepared to go. The paramedic told me that they had an injection of steroids that they could give me that would limit the swelling in my spinal cord and might have an impact on the extent of my injury. He said that it was not a guarantee, but wanted to know if I would like to have it. I told him, "Definitely." They determined that I should be airlifted by helicopter to Norfolk General Hospital. There was a heli-pad down the road at the Volunteer Fire Department and the ambulance would take me there. Since Becky could not go on the helicopter with me, they did not allow her to ride in the ambulance. With tears running down her face, Becky gave me a kiss. I did the only thing that I could think of at the moment, I told her, "I love you" and winked at her. She climbed out, the doors closed, and we were off.

The helicopter was waiting for us as we pulled up in front of the fire department. The paramedics transferred me into the chopper and we took off for Norfolk General. The helicopter crew consisted of a pilot and a paramedic who also served as the copilot. As we flew, I began to feel nauseous. It became increasingly obvious to me that I was going to throw up. I tried to get the attention of the paramedic, but the noise of the rotor blades was extremely loud and he had on headphones that allowed him to communicate with the pilot. With my weakened condition, I was not able to yell or generate much volume at all in my voice. I was lying flat on my back with my neck in a brace in my head strapped down. Desperately, I tried to catch his eye. I called out twice, but he could not hear me. My arms were strapped down and I'm not sure if I could have moved them even if they weren't. Before I could do anything else, I threw up. Since I was lying on my back there was no way for me to expel everything out of my mouth. Now I could no longer call out, I could not swallow what I had in my mouth and it was running in my nose. It was the first time that I truly feared for my life in this whole incident. I thought to myself that it would be terrible to have been saved from the water and then to choke to death as I was being airlifted to the hospital.

Time slowed down once again. As I tried to hold my breath, I was running out of air. My lungs began to burn once again. I tried to blow air out my nose to clear the passages but it didn't work. I could feel my eyes widening with fear. Just before I was about to give up hope, he looked back at me, saw what had happened and immediately tilted the stretcher and with his fingers cleared my mouth so I could breathe. As I was taking my first few breaths, he wiped my face off. I blew air out my nose to clear that out as well. The next thing I knew, we were landing atop the hospital and a team of doctors and nurses was headed towards the helicopter.

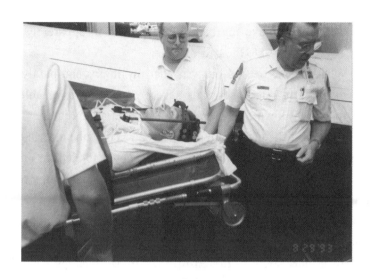

Chapter Five
Lesson #1

The medical team transferred me to a stretcher and rushed me to the hospital. I remember feeling the wind from the helicopter blades as we headed across the roof of the hospital. The doors opened and things started to move very quickly. I'm not sure exactly what happened but it didn't take too long before everything went black.

When I woke up, I was in a bit of a haze. My mind was cloudy because of the pain medications. I was in a hospital room by myself. I couldn't move anything at all. After a few seconds of trying to clear my head, I noticed that my breathing seemed weird. It took a quick look around to realize that there was a large tube running down my throat. Additionally, there was a small tube running up my nose. One of my nostrils was itchy,

27

but I could not move my hand up to scratch it, apparently my arms were strapped to the bed.

What I came to find out was that my injury had paralyzed my diaphragm. Because of its severe nature, I was unable to breathe on my own and they had put me on a ventilator. That was a large tube running down my throat. This tube allowed air to go in and out of my lungs but it prevented food from going down my throat. As a result, the small tube running up my nose was a feeding tube. Over the course of the next few days, some kind of blue mush was pushed up the tube and into my stomach. The color of it was a terrible looking bright blue and thus it was called "Smurf food". In retrospect, I'm very happy that the Smurf food was being pumped directly into my stomach because I can't imagine how nasty it must have tasted.

Much of what I'm about to tell you I was not actually aware of at the time. With all the medications I was in and out of consciousness on a regular basis. My family was allowed to visit me for 15 minutes at a time every couple of hours. There was a huge collection of family members and there was a very limited number that were allowed in. My parents and my sister were there, as were Becky and her parents. The list of other family members and friends is too long to write. I was aware of who was visiting my room, but did not realize exactly how many people were in the waiting area.

The ventilator provided an interesting challenge right from the beginning. Since it was blocking my throat, I was unable to speak. The only method of communication I had was blinking my eyes. It didn't take too long before we worked out a system of yes and no. They would ask me a question and if I blinked once the answer was yes and if I blinked twice the answer was no. It was a pretty simple setup, but it was fairly effective. Of course, it was only effective for yes or no questions.

The family came up with a good idea for communication. They put together a board with all of the letters from the alphabet on it. It was divided into two columns and three rows. The top left row would have the letters a through e, the middle left row would have f through j and so on. The object of the board was for me to spell out whatever I was trying to say. To start the process, I would roll my eyes in the direction where the letter was. If I rolled my eyes up to the left, the letter was in the first row of the left-hand column. Once we established what row the letter was in, they would simply move their finger across the row until they came to the desired letter and I would blink.

If this all sounds a little bit complicated, it's because it was. It was not a very easy process but everyone got excited about it because it was almost a game. In some ways, it was a little bit like charades. What letter is it going to be? The process was not very fast, to say the least.

The problem was that they were so intent on getting the letters that they would forget what letters they had correctly gathered. I was trying to be patient and understand that this process was as difficult for them as it was for me. When we got stalled halfway through a sentence I would start again with a new sentence that said, "w-r-i-t-e i-t d-o-w-n!" It made sense to me, but it never happened.

Most of the medical information being passed along by the doctors was being given to my family. I didn't have a good handle on what was going on. The fact is there was so much uncertainty that *nobody* seemed to have a great handle on the situation. I had broken my neck, but the extent of the injury was not known. There were questions about how severe the nerve damage was and how it was going to affect my physical abilities. However, the initial concern was staying alive. The main issues were breathing, nutrition, infection, pneumonia, neck stabilization and basic survival.

My initial few days after the injury were a blur. Through the drug-induced haziness, it was a constant cycle of wake and sleep punctuated by visits from the family and visits from the doctors and nurses and brief periods where nothing was happening at all.

Jonathan Carmichael, a friend of mine since I was young, was living in Norfolk. He came to visit a few times and brought me one of the most thoughtful gifts. As a Christian, there is nothing that is as valuable as promises from God. Jonathan put together a list of verses from the Bible that would serve as an encouragement to me. Since I was lying on my back, he put them on a poster board that could be mounted above my bed. He even made it double-sided so that I was not looking at the same verses all the time. During those times that nothing was going on I was able to enjoy God's promises to me.

The short visits that people were allowed to have were a real encouragement. They would come in and check on me. Even though I couldn't say anything, if I was able to catch someone's eye, I would wink at them just to let them know that I was okay. Years later, Mom told me that when I winked at her, I gave her an understanding that I was still the same me. I guess we never realize the impact of the little things that we do.

In retrospect, I realize that I may have made my family feel badly on occasion. The number of people that were allowed in the room at any given time was limited, so everyone was taking turns. The first question I had for my visitors was, "Where's

Becky?" It wasn't that I didn't enjoy being with my visitors, there was just something about her being there that made me feel better.

It was during one of those quiet times that I started to assess my situation. I could understand that I was going to have some physical limitations. My mind started to go back through some of the things that I had read over the course of my lifetime. An article from Reader's Digest popped into my memory and was a source of inspiration. It had talked about people with varying disabilities that needed assistance in their homes. Many of the things that they needed help with were not major items that would require a human helper. Instead, they would use a monkey to help them. The monkey could pick things up for them, help them move things, push buttons for them and just be a companion. I couldn't wait for my family to come so I could tell them about my idea.

We were still using the spelling board, so it was going to take a while to explain exactly what I was trying to get at. It was hard enough to get a sentence communicated by spelling out one letter at a time; now I was going to try and communicate an entire thought. It seemed like the process took forever. I think that they must have thought that I was losing it. The first sentence that I spelled out was, "I r-e-a-d a-n a-r-t-i-c-l-e i-n R-e-a-d-e-r-s D-i-g-e-s-t." There was excitement over the fact that they understood all the words in the sentence but then a bunch of questions popped up." Did you just read an article in Reader's Digest?" I blinked twice. "Are you excited because you can remember it?" I blinked twice again. "Do you remember when it was from?" Two more blinks. At that point, they started to talk among themselves about this article that I had read. Finally, someone turned to me and asked, "Can you tell us what it was about?" I'm not sure if my eyes lit up or not but I was very delighted to only blink once.

I was really hoping that this would work out. Really, from the time I was a little boy I had always wanted to have my own monkey. Doesn't every boy want a monkey? At first, I wasn't even interested in how useful a monkey could be; it was just the concept of how cool it would be. Everywhere I went, I would have a monkey sitting on my shoulder. I could become known as "the guy with the monkey". I could teach him to do all kinds of cool stuff.

When we were finally able to get information about the "Helping Hands" monkeys, the usefulness was even more evident. The monkey would be able to get things out of the refrigerator for me, to pick up things that I had dropped, to bring me things that I wanted and to provide companionship. All of these sounded exactly like what I needed.

Then we started to look at the fine print. The first point was that monkeys are not good around new people. That meant that I couldn't take the monkey out in public. It also meant that I could not have many new people come to visit me because it would upset the monkey. Also, monkeys are not good around children. They are known to bite so the people that train them take all their teeth out. The food that the monkeys eat has to be soaked in water so that they can "gum it". Somehow, the prospect lost all of its appeal when it moved into the real world.

After several days, I was stabilized enough to come off the ventilator. It was a major relief to be able to speak once again. Becky came to visit me by herself. It was the first time that I had a chance to really talk to her since the injury occurred. I was honestly worried about her and how she was holding up under all of the stress and pressure. On top of that I wanted to know how my injury was going to affect our relationship.

Over the past few days I had been thinking about a couple of things that I thought she needed to hear. "Becky," I told her, "I'm not sure what the future holds for me. It looks like there's going to be a lot of limitations and difficulties. I'm not sure how I am going to handle them, but I'm concerned about you as well. If these limitations and problems are going to be too much for you, it's okay if you decide to leave. One of my biggest concerns right now is for you to be okay. I need to be sure that you are not feeling overwhelmed."

I continued, "Besides that, I'm not sure what you are feeling towards me right now. If you are feeling pity or feeling sorry for me, that's not really what I want. Pity is no foundation for a relationship. I need you to be sure that you are aware of your own feelings." Then I said, "I've been thinking a lot about the people that we know. I don't want them to put any pressure on you. If you are only staying because of what people would say if you left, remember that they are not part of the two of us. Our relationship is between us and they don't have any say about that. If you are worried about people saying that you left me at my lowest point, don't worry about what they say. I just need you to be okay." I finished by saying, "There is a whole lot going on right now, I just don't want you to feel any undue pressure. At this point, I care very much about how you are doing. If you need to leave in order to take care of yourself, I understand. What is most important to me is your well-being."

At this point in time, Becky had tears streaming down her face. She told me, "I love you for who you are. Whether you can walk or not is not important to me. I love the man you are on the inside. If your injury has changed who you are on the inside, you're not the man that I thought you were. Besides, if you think you can get rid of me that easily, you have another thing coming."

I did not realize the full impact of what she was saying until much later. This conversation molded so much of my understanding about life with a disability. It impressed me with the simple fact that people still love me. Becky's statement had clearly demonstrated that the key to relationships is who you are internally. If I was going to have an impact in life, it was going to be based on my character, faith, and personality.

It really taught me the importance of having someone who loves you for who you are. I found out that I had such a person. What she had shown me about herself was absolutely amazing. It was then that I knew she was going to be the woman that I would marry.

The next step in my healing process was to install a "Halo". The purpose of the Halo was to keep my neck bones stable while they healed. Because the neck bones were broken, I had no way to support my head. They needed to install something that would provide support for my head as well as keep my neck from moving.

My Halo looked like it came straight out of the torture chamber. There was a plastic jacket with a wool liner that went around my chest. Four rods came up from the jacket, two in the front and two in the back. These rods attached to a metal semicircle that went around my head. This is the piece that gives the device its name. The worst part about the whole thing was that in order to use this device to hold my head still, they had to put four screws from the Halo into my skull. Two of the screws went into my forehead and the other two were attached to the back of my head.

The way that they installed the Halo was extremely simple and yet very disconcerting. Up until this point my head was held securely in place by a clamp that went to the top of the bed. The first thing that the doctors did was put the plastic jacket and lambswool on me. The nurse's aide undid the clamp and took my head in his hands. With so many broken bones in my neck, he was literally holding my life in his hands. A wrong move on his part and I would have been gone.

As the nurse's aide was holding my head, the doctor was lining up all the pieces. He got the rods in place, then attached the Halo headpiece. Once he had everything lined up like he wanted, he gave me a couple of numbing shots in the areas where he was going to attach the screws. When I was sufficiently numb, he started to thread the screws in. Even though I could not feel the screws going in, I could see the wrench turning them. After they got through the skin, I could hear a grinding noise as they tightened against the skull bone.

Once the Halo was installed, there were two other tasks that needed to be addressed. First, I needed to get up and out of bed. However, this was complicated by low blood pressure as a result of my injury. Whenever they would try to sit me up, even the slightest bit, I would begin to pass out. The answer was a reclining chair. They transferred me into a special chair with the back laid completely flat. Then they raised my head a little bit at a time. Once I got to the point that I was about to pass out, they would lay the head of the chair back again.

The second item on the list was figuring out where to go from here. There was a discussion about the best options available as far as Spinal Cord Rehabilitation. My parents were concerned that I receive the best possible care. They wanted to make sure that I was headed in the right direction from the very beginning. Among the options that we discussed were Craig Hospital in Denver, the Shepherd Center in Atlanta, the Miami Project and Thomas Jefferson University Hospital in Philadelphia.

The obvious choice was Thomas Jefferson University Hospital because it was so close to home. Dad, Mom and I talked about this decision as setting a foundation for the rest of my life. They were concerned that if we just went with what was close, it may not be of the same quality as what was available in other states.

After extensive discussion and a lot of prayer, we finally decided that we would go with Thomas Jefferson University Hospital. The understanding was that if there were any problems it was always possible to move to a different location. Plans were made so that I would be able to transfer to Thomas Jefferson as soon as I was medically stable.

The arrangements were for a "Life Flight" jet to take me from Norfolk to Philadelphia. Due to my medical condition and the concerns that they had for my life, the plane was given priority routing. My plane was actually given a direct flight route and had priority clearance second only to Air Force One.

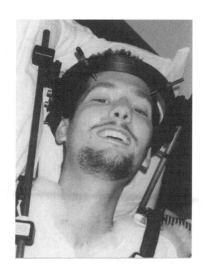

Chapter Six
My Neck is Stuck

The Life Flight arrived at the Northeast Philadelphia Airport. We were met by an ambulance which transported me to Thomas Jefferson University Hospital. Of course, the suspension on an ambulance is very tight anyway so I felt every single bump along the way. Since the screws from the Halo went right into my skull, it felt like every movement on the ambulance was transmitted directly to my bones.

Initially, I was granted a private room while they assessed my needs. The pressing issues were healing my broken neck bones, avoiding bedsores, and keeping me healthy. Keeping me healthy was just a matter of monitoring what I ate and watching for infection. The bedsores were easily preventable as well. The nursing staff was charged with repositioning me in the bed on a regular basis. The key issue then was getting my neck healed.

Doctors decided that they should do a bone graft. They took two pieces of bone from my hips and used them to create a stable base. They would then utilize stainless steel screws and some wire to tie everything together. The day that surgery was scheduled, I was sent down to the prep area for the operating room. They had given me a Valium so that I would be prepared and relaxed. In spite of that, I still was feeling a bit nauseous and queasy. They decided to delay the surgery until the following day. I was feeling quite apprehensive about what was going to happen.

Everything seemed to have calmed down by the next day so we went forward with the surgery. It was supposed to last for about eight hours, but it ended up taking well over ten hours to complete. They started by making an incision in the front of my throat and attaching the first bone graft and a few screws before turning me over and doing the same thing through an incision in the back of my neck. The difficulty was that during the surgery on the back of my neck, there was so much pressure that the graft in the front gave way. They had to turn me over and redo the work that had been done on the front. All in all, I ended up with the two bone grafts, a mess of wires and 11 stainless steel screws in my neck. It's definitely a weird thing to look at an x-ray of my neck and see where the 11 screws are.

Shortly after surgery, I was transferred from my private room into a four bed room. The man in the bed beside me was named Pablo. He was also a quadriplegic with an injury similar to mine. Our injuries had occurred around the same time and at the same level. Directly across from me was Roosevelt. He also was a quad, but his injury was a little bit higher than mine. In the bed beside him was Chucky. Chucky had a Traumatic Brain

38

Injury and some other physical disabilities that went with it. He did not say a whole lot.

Pablo's primary language was Spanish. I had studied a little bit of Spanish in high school and college, but it was not very good. Fortunately for him, it was just enough that when he was in trouble and could not talk to anyone else, I was able to at least ask him some questions that he was able to answer with a simple, "Si" or "No". His wife's name was Sylvia and she came in to visit him almost every day. She was very concerned about him, especially his weight. Although Pablo was slightly heavier than I was, Sylvia was always shaking her head and saying, "Pablo so skinny". She brought him food from home on a regular basis because the hospital food just did not suit his palate.

Pablo and I got along very well, especially when we were watching baseball. After visiting hours were over, there was not a lot to do in the evening. We passed the time by watching television. In 1993, the Phillies made the playoffs and advanced all the way to the World Series. As a fan of Philadelphia sports, I was used to a certain amount of futility. The Phillies had won the World Series in 1980 and the 76ers had won the championship in 1983, but apart from that, the city was not overflowing with championships. As much as I could remember those championships, I was really hoping for a new one.

Pablo and I enjoyed the excitement of the postseason. During the first playoff series, Pablo uttered a catchphrase that stuck with me. When things started to go bad, he would simply say to me, "Rob, Phillies, uh oh!" I would tell him that I thought they were going to come back, and often it worked out that way. Unfortunately, in game six of the World Series the Phillies brought in their closer, Mitch Williams. He was known as the "Wild Thing" and he sure lived up to his name. He had been struggling throughout the World Series and with the Phillies down three games to two, he came in to close out game six and take the series to a decisive game seven. Alas, as a true Philadelphia fan I understood the sheer agony and misery of defeat. "Wild Thing" delivered a ball down the middle to Joe Carter who promptly crushed the ball into the outfield seats for a home run. That was the end of the game, that was the end of the series, Pablo simply called over to me, "Rob, Phillies, uh oh."

Roosevelt was a different kind of person. He was very self-sufficient and very used to having things done his way. He came from the inner city and did not have a whole lot of patience or social grace. That basically boiled down to the fact that he was fairly abusive of the nursing staff. When they didn't do things like he wanted, he would holler at them. For that simple reason, they did not quickly respond to him when he hit the call bell. This presented a bit of a problem for our room. Roosevelt had what was called a sip and puff call bell. All he had to do to make it work was blow on it. Pablo and I had the regular style call bells and somehow we could never make them work when we wanted to. At one point, Pablo was fairly sick, feeling nauseous and in pain. On those nights, he would groan and make all kinds of noises in his bed. Because I was the only one that spoke Spanish, I would ask him if he needed the nurse. When he responded yes, I would not be able to ring my own call bell, so I would have to ask Roosevelt to ring his call bell for me. Because the nurses were mad at Roosevelt for the way that he had treated them during the day, they would basically ignore him. Then Roosevelt would get mad at them because Pablo was

40

groaning and complaining and obviously was in pain. He would ring his call bell repeatedly and the nurses would in turn get more irritated with him.

Roosevelt's relationship with his friends was unique as well. He didn't have very many visitors. With his outgoing personality, he usually latched on to my visitors. He couldn't remember everyone's name, so he just decided that he would call them by their relationship to me. My parents became "Mr. Rob's Dad" and "Mr. Rob's Mom". My sister, Rebekah, became "Mr. Rob's Sister" and Becky became "Mr. Rob's Wife", even though we weren't even engaged, much less married. Once he had your name, it was a dangerous proposition because you never knew what Roosevelt was going to say to you. Sometimes he would ask you to help him get a drink, sometimes he just wanted to say hello. It was just a matter of whatever he needed at the time was asked of whoever was available.

The only person that came to visit Roosevelt on a regular basis was his semi-girlfriend, Karima. Being from Philadelphia, both he and Karima added an "R" to the end of her name.

Becky had arranged to take all of her college courses as independent study for the fall semester, and she and Rebekah came in to visit every day. As a result, Karima got to know them fairly well. To her, it was easier to call both of them "Rebekah", but the Philadelphia accent put that extra "R" on the end. As a result, the two of them became known as the "Rebekars".

Unfortunately for Roosevelt, Karima did not come in for many (if any) of the family training sessions. Mom, Dad and the "Rebekars" were at the hospital every day and wanted to learn everything they could about my care. They were learning about how to position me, transfer me, help with my activities of daily living and how my bodily functions would change as a result of the injury. Karima didn't have this training so when Roosevelt had any issues, he had to explain to her exactly what he wanted done. Her lack of training and his lack of patience didn't give her a whole lot of self-confidence while she was helping him.

The most memorable occasion when this came into play was one night when Roosevelt was having some discomfort in his neck. When I first arrived at the hospital, he had been wearing a collar to keep his neck stabilized, but his neck was strong enough that he had been able to get rid of the collar. With the level of his injury, he was not able to move a whole lot. Somehow, as he was trying to move, his head slid down the side of the pillow and his neck was slightly bent. He called to Karima and told her, *"My neck is stuck!"* The conversation that followed after this was extremely comical. It didn't seem to matter what she asked, he just simply stated, *"My neck is stuck!"* Finally, he decided that she was going to have to sit him up and move him higher in the bed. Without proper training, Karima was left to follow his instructions. She sat him up on the side of the bed and got ready to reposition him. It was at this point that he had a leg spasm that she was not expecting. He started to slide down, off the side of the bed. The wheelchair that he used was sitting right beside the bed so she thought that the best thing might be to try to get him into the wheelchair so that he didn't fall on the floor. Unfortunately, she couldn't get any type of grip on him and her transfer technique was definitely not "textbook".

The two "Rebekars" were visiting me and as we watched, Karima tried a number of different ways to get him back up either into the bed or on to the wheelchair. The problem was that every time she did something, he would slide down another 2 inches. Finally, he had almost slid completely to the floor. Karima didn't know what else to do and so she hollered, "Rebekar! Help! I dropped him!" Between the three of them, they managed to get him back up into the bed. It served as a vital lesson to me just how important it is to understand how to take care of yourself and how to explain to others what you need.

I started to do some work in both physical and occupational therapy. In both instances, the major obstacle that I was facing was my strength. I had not moved very much since my injury and had lost the use of many of my muscles. I had absolutely no use of my legs and only partial use of my arms. The way I would describe it roughly is that I can use most of the muscles in my arms that are covered in areas that tan. For example, I can use my biceps, but not my triceps. I can use the muscles that draw my wrist up, but not the ones that pull my wrist down. They had a very cool chart that correlated the areas that I could feel with the level of my injury and the muscles that would be affected. As a result of that, the doctors and nurses were often doing assessments of what I could feel and what I could not feel. While that doesn't sound all that horrible, it is a bit more daunting when you realize that the testing is done with a safety pin. They would take the sharp end of a safety pin and lightly touch my skin asking, "Can you feel this?" At one point in time I suggested that someone use a permanent marker to draw a line showing exactly where I could feel. That way, I wasn't being retested and poked all the time.

Although my major concerns at Thomas Jefferson University Hospital were related to my health, I was in the physical therapy gym every day. My initial workouts were fairly discouraging. They would attach weights to my arms and have me simply do bicep curls. The weights only weighed a half pound or a pound and after a set of 10 reps I was completely exhausted.

Occupational therapy was much the same way. They were trying to teach me how to take care of myself all over again. The first step in the process was to learn how to feed myself. My wrists were not very strong and my hand strength was negligible. To keep everything in the proper position, they gave me wrist braces that had a pocket in the palm for silverware. Again, the strength issue was the primary problem. I simply did not have the strength to get the silverware from the table top to my mouth. An additional problem was the fact that the Halo limited my ability to move my head around. As a result, I could not look down far enough to see what was on the table in front of me.

The answer to the second problem came first. They gave me a piece of equipment called "prism glasses". "Prism glasses" are triangular pieces of glass on an eyeglass frame. The effect is that as you look into them, they show you what is straight down in front of you. So as I looked forward, I was able to see everything on the table in front of me. Seeing the tabletop and figuring out how to coordinate my movements in this altered perspective were two very different things.

The strength problem was handled differently. They set up a pulley system over my head. A string came down from a pulley and attached to my right arm. That string connected to another pulley behind my back and then to a counterweight. They would put five or so pounds of counterweight on the pulley system to give me additional help. Now the struggle became twofold. First, I had to struggle to pull down on the string to reach the tabletop. Then, I had to work hard to bring the fork or spoon back to my mouth.

The first few times that we tried this method, it was a "dry run". Although I was giving it all I had, there was no way to actually track if I was accomplishing anything. My therapist decided that we would try to use some real food. The problem was that I had just had surgery on my neck and I also had pancreatitis—a complication from the injury. As a result, all of the food that I was eating had to be puréed. She figured that pudding would be a very good compromise. I like pudding because it was sticky and I could make it stay on my spoon without sliding off. The first day that I set out to feed myself pudding was a disappointment, at least to me. I struggled for 30 minutes just to get my spoon near the pudding. That day, I never got anything near my mouth at all.

The next day, it was back to the same thing. This time, there was a little bit more success. It didn't take me nearly as long to get some pudding on the spoon, but I still did not have the strength to get it up to my mouth. After a few days work, I was getting stronger and more adept at filling my spoon, but I was still struggling to actually feed myself. It was at the end of one of my therapy sessions that I was determined to make this work. I had half a spoonful of pudding that had been on the spoon for over 15 minutes. I was getting it up almost to my mouth, but I was still an inch or two away from my target. It was very difficult because I knew that all I needed to do was lean over an inch or two to reach "the prize" but the Halo would not allow any movement. As I pulled the spoon towards my mouth, my muscles shook with exertion but I just couldn't make it. My therapist asked if I was ready to be done for the day. I told her I wanted to rest for a second and give it one more shot.

After a minute or so, I made my last effort of the day. I was closer than I had ever been and I was determined to make this work. I pulled as hard as I could and the spoon reached my mouth! I fed myself a spoonful of warm, instant, institutional vanilla pudding and it just might have been one of the sweetest things that I had ever eaten in my entire life. It was a major sense of accomplishment and proof that hard work does have its rewards.

The next project I worked on in occupational therapy was my handwriting. Having lost most of the function in my hand and wrist, I had to learn how to write all over again. Now, instead of using the fine motor movement in my fingers, I had to learn how to write with my shoulder. My whole arm moved the pen, rather than just my fingers. Becky's birthday is near the end of September. I decided that I would like to compose a poem and write it in the birthday card that I had for her. It was quite a challenge to make it work. The poem was only six lines long but it was so physically demanding for me to write it that it actually took four days of work in therapy to get the poem written.

Among the lessons I learned was the difference between caretakers. I had two nurses at Thomas Jefferson both named Kathy. Actually, one was named Kathy and the other was named Cathy. Kathy was a very caring nurse. In addition to her work at the hospital, she was also the team nurse for the Philadelphia Phillies. Kathy was very positive and upbeat, but also provided a very realistic outlook. I was still taking medication for pain, which Kathy said was very addictive. Of course, when I wanted a shot of pain medication, I would ask them to shoot it in my leg. The great part about not being able to feel my leg was that the injection did not hurt at all. Kathy

46

decided that I may have been getting addicted. Her idea was to give me my shots where I could feel them. The logic was that if I was in a tremendous amount of pain, I would be willing to take the small amount of pain from the injection to get relief. In hindsight, I understand the wisdom of her idea. The difficulty was that it didn't work out exactly as she had planned. On my left arm, right on the line between where I can feel and where I can't feel there is a strip of sensation that is always tingly. I would describe it as almost a sensation of being asleep, but all the time. I don't know if Kathy knew that spot existed or if it just happened by chance, but every time she would give me my pain medication, she hit that exact area. It hurt very badly, but she had challenged my manhood and I felt like I could not tell her that it hurt. The very rapid result was that she only had to do that twice before I decided that I didn't need any more pain medication shots.

Cathy, on the other hand, was a little rough around the edges. She was full of attitude. In addition to her exceptionally long hair, which was usually held in place with just a headband, she had long nails painted bright pink. She also wore a fair bit of jewelry, at least one or two necklaces and rings on most of her fingers. She didn't seem to think that any of these items might interfere with her ability to work cleanly. Her attitude was that everyone in the hospital was beneath her and she was definitely smarter than everybody.

It seemed like anytime anyone asked her for anything, she would explain to them why they didn't need it or why she shouldn't have to get it for them. One evening I was not feeling well, complaining about a nauseous stomach. When I asked Cathy for something to settle my stomach, she promptly informed me, "You can't feel your stomach!" Sarcastically, I thanked her and told her that I was feeling much better now that I realized that I couldn't feel my stomach. When I lost my lunch later in the evening, there was a certain delightful irony in the fact that she was the nurse that had to clean things up. It was the first lesson that I learned in making sure that I didn't let people define what I could and couldn't do.

I received a number of very thoughtful and kind gifts while I was in the hospital. There were two in particular that I really appreciated. I'm not even sure who was the original point of contact on this, but I received a personal letter from both Joni Erickson Tada and Dennis Byrd. The letter from Joni was very uplifting and spoke about dealing with loss and living with difficult circumstances. The letter from Dennis Byrd was very inspirational. Dennis had been a professional football player for the New York Jets. He broke his neck on the field of play and was told that he would never walk again. Dennis took this diagnosis as a challenge and began to do everything in his power to strengthen his muscles and overcome the circumstances he found himself in. He had written a book entitled "Rise Up and Walk". With a combination of faith and determination, Dennis was able to walk out of the rehabilitation facility at the end of his therapy. He refused to be defined by his injury or limited by his circumstances.

His message struck home with me and I began to dedicate myself to overcoming my injury. At night when I was by myself I would concentrate on my big toe. I would will it to wiggle. After a number of nights of working and willing, I began to wonder if the problem was my faith was not strong enough. I was praying to God for help to make my toe move, but nothing was happening. For some reason He was not answering me. It must have been because I was not trying hard enough. Maybe it was because I did not have enough faith. Maybe I was not concentrating hard enough or did not have enough determination. I redoubled my efforts, concentrating, praying and thinking "wiggle thoughts", but nothing happened.

After I became almost completely frustrated, I came to the simple realization that the nerves that ran from my brain to my toe were no longer connected. I could pray and will and hope and work as much as I wanted to, the issue was that I could not regrow the nerves just by thinking about it. It finally came to me that I was not going to "overcome" my injury. Nothing short of a miracle was going to reconnect the nerves. No, I was not going to be able to determine myself into walking, the test that lay in front of me was how I was going to live my life with the limitations that I had.

The message that Dennis Byrd had put out there was work hard and you will overcome your obstacles. I came to understand that his message was excellent in some circumstances but did not necessarily apply to mine. The lesson that I learned was work hard to do everything you can in spite of the obstacles and limitations that you face.

As I began to get healthier, it was time for me to move out of the acute care setting at Thomas Jefferson University Hospital and on to a rehabilitation center. My family and I had not been overly impressed with the care that I was receiving at Thomas Jefferson and revisited the conversation we had in the hospital in Norfolk. We talked about other rehabilitation centers that might be better suited for me. The next move in the Thomas Jefferson University system was ten Philadelphia city blocks away to

Magee Rehabilitation Hospital. I said that if Magee was just going to be more of what we were getting at Thomas Jefferson, I was not interested in going.

My parents decided to take a field trip over to Magee to see how things were. When they returned, they were full of energy and excitement about what was going on over there. I decided to take their word for it and transfer. We did have the understanding that if there was any problem, I could move to a different spinal cord center.

Chapter Seven
Not If, When

The move from Thomas Jefferson to Magee was something like a move from night to day. Somehow, my room at Thomas Jefferson was always dark. There were few windows and the entire facility felt old. At Magee, my new room had windows and I was fortunate enough to get a bed by the window. Now, the view that I had was not amazing, I got to look straight across the street at an office building but it did allow me to see the sunshine..

I was still wondering about whether or not this was the best place for me. Would I be treated the same as I had been at Thomas Jefferson? It didn't take very long for those questions to be answered. When I arrived at my room, I met Kim Riley, my daylight shift nurse. On top of being very well-informed about spinal injury, Kim was pleasant and fun. She explained a lot of the issues that I was going to be facing in a very plain and simple way that did not speak down to me. She didn't mind talking with me, not to me or at me. In a very subtle way it was the start of life being fun again.

The other person that changed my life was Beth Adams. She was my occupational therapist. The first day that I went down to the occupational therapy gym I was completely blown away by what she said to me. The first question out of her mouth was, "So, what do you want to do?" That definitely wasn't what I was expecting. I told her, "You know the level of my injury and you know what I'm capable of." I explained, "If you can set the goals for me, I will work very hard to achieve them." Beth told me what I was able to accomplish was completely dependent upon me. She said that if I was interested in doing something, I would be able to accomplish it. I may not do it exactly like I used to, I may not do it exactly like everyone else, I may not do it exactly like I want to but I would be able to do it. It was almost like I opened my eyes for the very first time when she explained this. My mentality completely shifted. Now, instead of thinking about accomplishment as "ifs" I was starting to look at them as "whens". It wasn't if I was going to finish my schooling, it was when. It wasn't a matter of if I was going to drive again, it was when. It wasn't a matter of if I was going to get married, it was a matter of when. It wasn't a matter of if I was going to get a job and support my family, it was a matter of when. I'm pretty sure that she has no idea exactly how much of an impact her question had upon my life.

Beth had an intern that worked with her named Jennifer. She worked with me one-on-one during my first weeks at

Magee. This gave her an opportunity to develop her own care plan and set of goals for me.

One of the interesting things I learned during occupational therapy was that the majority of patients with spinal cord injuries found that their dominant side was usually the weaker side after the injury. For some reason, if you are right-handed before the injury, the muscles in your left arm were stronger than the muscles in your right arm following injury. For some reason, I was fortunate enough to be in the 10% where my dominant hand was still my much stronger hand. My injury affected the cervical area of my spine at the C5-C6 level. In my instance, the C5 level was on my left hand, the C6 level was on my right hand. Although I would not say that my rehab was easy, it made it a little bit easier because I did not have to learn how to do everything with my opposite hand.

The primary thing that I had to work on was called tenodesis. With the limited use of my hands and arms, I could not effectively grasp things in my hands. The only movement that I had in my wrist was the ability to draw my hand up. The natural physiological response to that is for my hand to draw into a fist. By working to strengthen muscles, I was able to develop a pinching motion between my thumb and index finger. Jennifer told me that it would be very difficult at first, but then with practice I would be able to refine my abilities to the point where I could pick up change off the countertop. I figured that she knew what she was talking about, but it was a pretty difficult task that was set out for me.

One of the fun things about all the visitors that I had was that they brought me snacks. I had lined the entire windowsill of my room with a variety of delicious treats. Jennifer asked me to bring some of them down for practice with tenodesis. Her idea was that I would be able to reward myself whenever I picked anything up. It sounded like a plan to me, so the first day I brought down a bunch of M&Ms. They sat on the tray in front of me and as I tried to pick them up, I had no success at all. Instead of pinching them between my thumb and finger, I was merely pushing them around the tray. As various members of the staff walked by, they asked me how I was doing. As I explained that I had not been able to pick any of them up, they would grab a couple of M&Ms and pop them in their mouth. I asked, "Hey, can you give me one of those?" The answer came back quickly, "Sure, just pick one up." By the end of the hour-long therapy session, I had not picked up a single M&M.

When it was time for occupational therapy the next day, I knew that I needed to bring something other than M&Ms. I decided that Swedish Fish would fit the bill. The good news about Swedish Fish is that they don't slide around as easily as the M&Ms. The unfortunate thing is that they don't stick up that high and they are still difficult to get a hold of. About halfway through my session, I still had not picked up a single thing. It was then that my ingenuity kicked in. I realized that if I licked the side of my hand that the Swedish Fish would stick to it. I ate a couple that way before anyone noticed and accused me of cheating. Jennifer outlawed Swedish Fish as a result, but it taught me I could accomplish things if I was willing to work at it and develop alternative strategies. It wasn't exactly following the rules, but it did have the desired effect and I thoroughly enjoyed my snack.

Jennifer came up with a variety of activities that were fun. One of our therapy days was a game of "Pitching Pennies". I was competing against two other quads to see who would win. The fact is that we were all relatively young and male which meant that it was going to be a competition. Much to my chagrin, I lost miserably. It wasn't necessarily the fact that they were better than me, it was just the fact that our injuries were at different levels which meant they had a little bit more hand function than I did. Needless to say, I was not real happy about the outcome.

I was having trouble with low blood pressure. It was running around 90/60. Considering that the usual blood pressure is 120/80, that is pretty low. For some reason, my blood pressure seemed to bottom out right after lunch. This, unfortunately, coincided with the time that I went occupational therapy. When my blood pressure dropped, I would start to gray out. It would start with gray spots in the middle of my vision. Those spots would get bigger and bigger until I could barely see at all. Beth used to joke about the fact that she could tell when my blood pressure was dropping because the color would drain out of my face. The only way to get the blood flowing back to my brain and to keep me from losing consciousness was to tilt my chair back so that I was in a reclining position. After sitting like this for a few minutes, my blood pressure would usually pick up enough so that I would not pass out. The sad part about this was that it usually took just long enough to ruin my therapy session. Beth would tell me that if she didn't know that I liked her, she would start to think that I was just trying to get out of my occupational therapy.

A few weeks after I arrived at Magee I was able to get passes to leave the hospital for short periods of time. The first time I ever got to go home after my injury was on a Friday night. I was still wearing the Halo and the only way for me to get home was to ride in my parents' station wagon. The whole idea of doing a transfer into a car is not fun at all. I am 6' 2" and my legs are not real long which means that I have a very long torso. The bars that held the Halo stuck up a few inches above my head. The long and short of it is that when I was sitting in the car the bars of the Halo were basically touching the roof of the car. When I arrived home, we went to get out of the car and the problem was that they could not figure out how to get the Halo bars down low enough to get me through the door of the vehicle and back out in a wheelchair. It didn't seem to matter what direction they turned, twisted or pulled, there was just no way to get my head down low enough to get me out of the vehicle.

The first progress we made was getting the front two bars out. Now the issue was that the back bars were sticking on the doorframe and I was stuck half in and half out of the vehicle. Of course, in this particular instance it had to be raining. I was sitting in the back seat of the vehicle which further complicated issues. What we ended up doing finally was moving my backside about halfway across the seat, then bending my head down and sliding me back to the edge of the seat once my head was already down. It wasn't pretty, but it worked. Thank goodness that vinyl seats made it easy to slide.

Over the course of the next few weeks, the trips home got a little bit easier. We finally decided that Becky's Cavalier was probably easiest to use for transporting. It was a two door which meant that the door openings were bigger and there was more room to maneuver. One evening as we were headed back to the hospital, I wasn't feeling very well and she was concerned about what was going on. We were hurrying back and encountered traffic. My suggestion was to paint "Ambulance" backwards on my forehead and hang my head out the window while my sister Rebekah hollered siren noises. I would like to say that I was delirious from being sick, but the fact is that my sense of humor is just that bad.

The medical staff at Magee was very high on the concept of "The Cure". A few of the doctors there were on the very cutting edge of spinal cord injury research. They had explained at some of our educational sessions just what was going on. The overall sense of progress was that there would be a cure for spinal cord injury in the next three to five years. A few of my roommates decided that this sounded like a good idea. What they would do was go home, get the clicker, watch TV and wait for the cure. It was almost like they were hitting the pause button on life until "The Cure" came. While the concept of "The Cure" was very interesting to me, I did not feel that I could wait around for it. There was too much life to live in the meantime. Just because I could not engage life exactly as I had previously did not mean that I wasn't engaged. Whatever the circumstances were, I was alive and had the full opportunity to enjoy what was going on around me.

The guys that were willing to put their lives on hold were really missing something very important. Even though their lives were on pause, the lives of their friends, family and loved ones were not. Their girlfriends were not going to wait around until "The Cure" came. Their friends were not going to wait until "The Cure" arrived. Life was happening all around them, they were just excluding themselves from it.

One of the people that I met at Magee was a fellow patient named Paul. What I saw in him caused me no end of concern and puzzlement. Paul was a good young man. He had sung in the choir at church and been an active member of his church for as long as he could remember. One day as Paul was walking down the street on his way home from school, he was shot three times. There was no reason or explanation for it, he just ended up as the victim of a senseless crime.

His injury was much lower than mine; he had full use of his arms and fair bit of control of the muscles in his chest and abdomen. The difficulty he had was that one of the bullets had punctured his lung and significantly decreased his lung capacity. This injury also gave him some pain in his chest and made it difficult for him to move his right arm in a full range of motion.

Paul was really stuck on the fact that there was no explanation for what happened to him. He couldn't understand, in the immortal words of Nancy Kerrigan, "Why me?" The first time I met Paul, he gave me the whole story of what happened to him and how it just didn't make any sense. It wasn't fair, it was just wrong. After listening to his entire story, I tried to point out to him that he had so much going for him. He still had full use of his arms, there were a lot of things that he could still do, he had a clear mind and he was still a living, breathing person.

In a number of ways I was envious of Paul. He was able to push his own manual wheelchair. Paul was able to do a weight shift on his own. His hands were fully functional and he could play the piano beautifully. I had never really been able to play that well. Now, with the limitations in my hands, I was not able to play at all. It frustrated him that he was able use his hands to play but was not able to work the pedals on the piano without the use of his legs and feet.

Paul was also able to transfer himself in and out of bed. It was not easy for him because of the muscle limitations in his chest but he could do it. Having to rely on someone else to get me in and out of bed was frustrating. Paul had the ability to help himself but was not willing to do it because of the discomfort he felt. As I watched him refuse to work I was thinking to myself that I would love to be able to do what he could.

When the therapist came to teach Paul some skill building activities for getting up in the morning Paul gave them so much grief that it sounded like they had brought a cattle prod with them. Paul whined and complained about every single thing. In order to get dressed, he had to move himself around in bed. He would holler at the therapist that he was not able to do this. "I was shot, I'm severely injured." The fact is that his injury had occurred a few months prior. His wounds were all healed, the difficulty was that his muscles were not strengthened enough. The only way to get this done was to work hard, practicing the activities he would need to be able to do in order to take care of himself. Paul had put himself in a Catch-22 situation. He couldn't take care of himself because he was not strong enough. He wasn't going to get any stronger if he would not try to do something to help himself.

It took me a long time to come to grips with what was going on with Paul. As part of my treatment plan I went to see the psychologist once a week to talk about what was going on. I explained the whole Paul situation to her and expressed my frustration and lack of understanding. I talked to Beth about what was going on and asked her if she had any insight for me. Carol Ann, my physical therapist, did not have any insight for me either. It finally came to me that he was unable to deal with the future because he was having too much trouble dealing with the past.

By the time I finally came to somewhat of an understanding of the situation, Paul was of the opinion that my questions to the staff were biasing everyone against him. Whenever anyone pushed him to try harder, he blamed it on the fact that I had been talking to that person about him and they could not understand his perspective because of the information that I was telling them. It was at this point in time that Paul finally quit. He and his family decided that because nobody in the hospital would listen to him about the extent of his injury, he was better off at home.

I was still scratching my head about the whole situation when Beth finally explained it to me. The fact is that rehab is much harder for guys that have more function. They see the kind of breaks that a quad like me gets, the amount of help that I receive, and they want to be a quad too. Instead, they have to do for themselves. Nobody helps them to get dressed, they have to get dressed on their own. Nobody is going to carry their lunch tray, they have to figure out how to carry it themselves. From my perspective, they have a lot more freedom and ability than I do. From their perspective, they are stuck doing everything themselves. The fact is that freedom and independence comes at a price. Being independent means not relying on other people. The upshot of that is, you have to do as much as you can for yourself.

Once I understood this, it changed the way I looked at things. I began to wonder about what I could do for myself. The fact was that I would need help from people. The choice that I had to make was how much help I would actually need.

My first attempt to do something without depending on help from other people was addressing the elevators. I could get to the elevator but I could not press the buttons. Instead of having to rely on somebody coming along and pushing the buttons for me, I wanted to figure out how to do this myself. With the help of one of the occupational therapists, I was able to develop what I called an "elevator button pusher". It was really quite a simple tool. There were two flaps that wrapped around my hand to hold it on and there was a point that came out to push the button.

I was very pleased with my invention and could not wait to try it out. I carried the "elevator button pusher" on my lap as I made my way to the elevator. When I arrived at the elevators, I realized that I was going to have to get in the right position to reach the button. After carefully positioning my wheelchair, I was able to put my "pusher" on and hit the button. My invention slid right off the button. The problem was that it was plastic and the button was plastic and there was no friction. I was very bummed.

Not to be defeated, I decided that there had to be some way to fix this. I woke up in the middle of the night with a "Eureka" moment, a pencil eraser! The next day in occupational therapy I got a pencil eraser and placed it on the end of my "pusher". After therapy, I made my way down the hall, got myself in position, and tried out my invention. It worked!

It was not as efficient as the way that everyone else did it, but I did it on my own. That was the beginning of my realization that I was able to accomplish things if I would only put my mind to it. Beth had already told me, it was not going to look like everyone else, it was not going to be exactly like how I used to do it, but I could do it. It helped me to understand that just because someone can help you and just because they are willing to help you doesn't mean that you can't do it yourself. It may be fairly juvenile, but there is a tremendous amount of joy that comes from the fact that I did it by myself.

Chapter Eight
Home Again

Leaving Magee and becoming an independent individual was a multistep process. Towards the end of my stay a discharge plan was put together. It was determined that I would need a power wheelchair. The hottest new wheelchair on the market at that time was a Permobil. It was a front wheel drive which meant that it went well in all kinds of terrain and weather. It also had a number of power seat functions which meant that I could adjust the position of my seat to alleviate pressure. The wheelchair sounded great and we ordered it.

The problem was that the company is based in Sweden and in order to make sure that each wheelchair is properly fitted for the individual, they are basically custom-made. This process takes a long time. It took over two months after my discharge for my wheelchair to be delivered.

In the meantime, I was in a manual chair. As a result, I was basically immobile. I didn't have the strength to move myself around at all so it was up to other people to push me around. Okay, the truth is that I could push myself a little bit. The problem with pushing myself is that my right arm is stronger than my left arm and what would happen is I would go around in circles. In trying to be slightly independent, I would move myself but then it would end up just being completely frustrating.

My parents were renovating their home to make it accessible, but were not completely finished at the time of my discharge. Becky's parents had put an accessible room for me on the first floor of their home. They turned their den into a bedroom and added a roll-in shower. I went to live there while the work was finished on Mom and Dad's place.

During my stay there, Becky and I made everything official. After we went out for dinner one evening I asked her if she would be willing to share the rest of her life with me as my wife. She said yes and I was thrilled. We had to celebrate and the most fun thing we could think of was Italian cannolis. We picked up a dozen, then headed home to tell everybody the good news.

Now that we were planning our life together, a lot of pieces needed to be put in place. All of the "ifs" that came up during my occupational therapy had to become realities. I needed to be able to support Becky and that meant I needed to finish my education. I needed to get around so that meant I was going to have to learn how to drive again.

The driving part was going to be interesting. I wanted to get going on the process as quickly as possible. The problem was that the drivers training facility that was closest to me had a very long waiting list. Besides that, they had a process that would take a number of months to teach me how to drive. Their plan was to take me driving once a week until I was able to drive properly.

We found out about the drivers training program out in Hershey. There were two very good things about their program. First, it was only a week long. I would start on Monday and finish the program by taking my test at the Department of Motor Vehicles on Friday. Second, they were actively looking for people to participate in their program. My drivers training was funded by the Office of Vocation and Rehabilitation. They were in a bit of a financial pinch which is why the waiting list at the first training center was so long. Apparently, they had paid up front for a vehicle for the Hershey Medical Center and so Hershey was providing their drivers training at no charge until the cost of the vehicle was "paid off" in training hours. This worked out very well for me and so I was off to Hershey to learn how to drive again.

When I arrived for my initial consultation, I was very worried. I came into the office and met the driving instructor, Paul Goss. He didn't smile, he didn't laugh, he looked like he was bothered by the fact that we were there. The evaluation was fairly straightforward. He asked me to raise my right arm, raise my left arm, move my right hand around in a circle and then he was done. He simply said, "I can teach you to drive."

The driving instruction took place at an old abandoned airport in Hershey. It worked out very well because the runway offered a long stretch of paved road that did not have any traffic. Mr. Goss drove to the airport. Once we were there, he set me up behind the wheel. He put a "tri-pin" on the steering wheel and another one on a lever that controlled the gas and brake. A "tri-pin" is a brace that has a pin that you wrap your hand around and two more pins that go on either side of your wrist. I put my left hand in the "tri-pin" to control the gas and brake and my right hand in the one on the steering wheel. Mr. Goss gave me a quick lesson in how everything worked and told me to go forward.

I was scared to death. I put the brake on and shifted the van into "Drive". Very gingerly and slowly I began to let the brake off. The van began to roll down the runway. I didn't hit the gas, I was content to let the van coast. When we got to the middle of the runway, it started to go uphill a little bit and the van began to slow down. Mr. Goss told me to "give it a little gas." I tried to do a "little" but that didn't work out very well. When I hit the gas, the van lurched forward. My immediate reaction was to hit the brakes. The problem was that I couldn't do a "little" there either. Thankfully, Mr. Goss had the emergency instructor brake button in his hand and stopped the vehicle. Unfortunately, the instructor brake only had an on and off. It did stop the vehicle, but it brought us to a screeching halt.

This was my very first time driving using hand controls and I was doing a terrible job. I asked him if he thought I was going to be able to actually do this. He told me that he would have me driving 40 miles an hour by the end of the day. I was not so sure about that.

After I composed myself again, we practiced gently applying the gas and brakes. We went back and forth on the runway for the next hour and a half. Everything still seemed to be happening very fast and I was feeling like I was on the edge of losing control at all times. I was concentrating very hard on watching the "road", trying to avoid the potholes and to make sure there was enough room for turns and stops. As I made my trip down the runway, pushing the extent of my comfort zone, Mr. Goss told me to look down at the speedometer. Very cautiously, I glanced away from the road for a second to see that we were doing 42 mph. I was amazed. It showed me that he knew exactly what he was doing and if he thought that I could do this, I could definitely do it.

By the end of the week I was out driving around on the roads of Hershey and Harrisburg, not feeling extremely confident but feeling comfortable enough to keep up with traffic. I did have the advantage of already knowing how to drive—I got my license almost on the day of my 16th birthday. I could judge braking distance and turning radius so it was just a matter of learning how to use the equipment in his van.

Friday was the big day. I was slightly insulted as they made me take my written drivers exam again. After all, I had a spinal cord injury, I had not lost my mental faculties. However, if that's what they wanted, that's what I was going to. Mr. Goss stressed to me that if he put all of the effort into training me and then I messed up on the written part of the exam he was not going to be happy. I thought that he was not happy as it was and could not imagine him being less happy. Thankfully, everything went perfectly fine and I was able to pass both the written and driving part of my license exam.

Now came the fun part. The Office of Vocation and Rehabilitation was going to help with funding for a vehicle. They would not fund it until I had received my license. They figured that it would be stupid to fix up a vehicle for someone who was not able to drive. I had thought that the wait for my power wheelchair was long, but I had no idea how long the wait was going to be for the van. I passed my drivers exam during the first week of September and we had everything set to go for the van to be modified.

There were a few steps to the process. First, the floor of the van needed to be lowered so that I could see out the windshield. Next, they needed to put in a lift so that I would be able to get in and out of the vehicle. Finally, they needed to put in the gas and brake controls as well as a computer that would control the operations of the van. I was told that the van would be ready sometime in December, but it was not actually finished until April.

In the meantime, I started back to school. Before my injury I was a psychology major. Having seen a psychologist on a regular basis during my rehabilitation, I now had a much clearer understanding of the value of what I was studying. I became "a psychology major with purpose".

I only took three classes my first semester back. With the limitations on my hands, I was not able to take notes. The "Special Student Services" department provided me with carbonless paper. I had to find a fellow student who would be willing to use it in each of my classes. When they took their notes it would copy right onto the paper underneath and I would be able to take that second set of notes home with me. This meant that I had to pay attention in class because it is really hard to study from somebody else's notes.

I had to use someone else to write the exams for me. I would dictate, they would write. This meant that I would take the tests at a separate time from the rest of the students. It was very difficult for my scribes in these situations because I was getting them to write down equations and essay answers for classes that they had never taken. My exam helpers were absolutely wonderful and one of the reasons that I did well on my essay tests was because their handwriting was beautiful.

We scheduled our wedding for the end of my first semester back. Becky was finishing up her psychology degree in December and had a job lined up. We decided to get married over the Christmas break, on December 30. I finished my schooling in Philadelphia and headed out to McKeesport for the wedding. We were going to be living in McKeesport and I was set to start at the University of Pittsburgh as soon as we arrived home from our honeymoon.

Chapter Nine
Walking Together

Becky and I were both looking forward to our honeymoon, a tropical cruise. It was going to be our first experience of being a couple, living independently. Up to this point, we were surrounded by family and friends all the time. This was going to be an opportunity to spend a little time as just the two of us.

The morning after our wedding, we left bright and early. Actually, it was early but it was not bright at all. It was still dark because we had to be at the airport by 6:30 a.m. The cruise was leaving from San Juan, Puerto Rico, so we flew from Pittsburgh to Atlanta to San Juan.

I guess I need to explain how I get in and out of an airplane. My wheelchair is too wide to fit down the aisles of the airplane so they have what is called an Aisle Chair. The Aisle Chair is designed to take you down the aisle to your seat. It is not designed for comfort, it is not designed for style. Its only job is to get you onto the plane and to your seat.

If you have ever seen one of the dollies that a porter uses to carry luggage, you will understand the basic concept of the Aisle Chair. It is about the same width as one of those dollies, about the same size as one of those dollies and only has two wheels at the back like one of those dollies. The only difference is that where the luggage usually goes there is a small seat. There are two seatbelts that cross over your chest to hold you in place.

The way that they got me into the Aisle Chair was by brute force. Two baggage handlers would pick me up. One would grab underneath my arms and the other would grab under my knees. They would just hoist me from one seat to the next. There were two problems with this transfer method. The first was not a major problem; my shirt would get untucked. The second one was a big problem. Every time they would pick me up this way my pants would slide down about half an inch in the back. While this doesn't seem like a big problem, if you count the transfers it gets to be more of an issue. Transfer number one, from my wheelchair to the Aisle Chair. Transfer number two, from the Aisle Chair to my seat. After we arrived in Atlanta, transfer number three went from my seat back into the Aisle Chair. Transfer number four took me into a regular push wheelchair that they could take through the airport so we could reach our connecting flight. Transfers number five and six were into the Aisle Chair and then into my seat. Once we arrived in Puerto Rico, transfers number seven and eight were getting me back out of my seat and into a manual wheelchair that they could take down to the baggage area where my wheelchair was supposed to be waiting. Needless to say, the folks in Puerto Rico got to see more of me than they really wanted to.

My wheelchair was not in the baggage claim area as we were expecting. So we waited. It felt like a long time before the wheelchair arrived and when it did, we immediately noticed a problem. A wire was tied to the right arm rest of my wheelchair. I asked what it was and the man pushing my chair said that it had fallen off during the flight. They did not know where it went, but they thought that it was important enough that we should have it.

Becky and I have very different styles of handling situations like this. My reaction was to ask if anyone knew where it came from. As you can guess, no one had any idea. I asked if anyone in the airport would be able to help us get it fixed. Again the answer was that no one was really able to do that. It was at this point Becky decided to step in. She explained to them in no uncertain terms that we were on our honeymoon, we had a boat to catch and they better fix it because they had broken it. I don't admit this easily, but her approach seemed to strike a chord with them.

I will remind you that we were married on Friday, December 30, 1994. What that meant in this situation was that not only was it a Saturday, but it was also New Year's Eve. Even if it had been a weekday, all of the wheelchair repair shops on the island would have been closed. A few of the airport employees took my wheelchair to a service room in the airport to see what they could do with it. I will also remind you that we were in San Juan, Puerto Rico. This meant that everybody there spoke Spanish. I understand a little, teeny bit of Spanish, but Becky does not understand any.

It was at this point I realized that having your independence and being on your own has its plusses and minuses. This was truly our first time being on our own. There were no family members there to provide backup, there were no friends in the area, there was not a backup hospital facility, it was just us, by ourselves in a place far, far from home where everybody spoke a different language. On top of that, all we could do was sit in the hallway outside this room and wait to see what they could come up with.

After an hour and a half, they brought my wheelchair back out. I'm not sure exactly how they found out where the piece came from, but they did. It was reattached and my wheelchair was good to go again. Becky took the opportunity on transfer number nine to make sure that my pants were properly repositioned.

Becky had done a lot of research for our cruise. She had made to the company aware of our situation. As a result, they arranged for an accessible van to pick us up at the airport and drive us to the docks. She had done a lot of checking to ensure that the cruise ship was accessible as well. Everything seemed to be in very good order as we got in the van and headed over to the docks.

When we arrived at our destination, I went to turn my wheelchair on and get out of the van. The problem was that when I hit the button to turn the chair on, nothing happened. The lights that should have come on did not. As a matter of fact, nothing happened at all. Now, we were stuck in a van, at the docks in Puerto Rico. The driver and his assistant were very nice and tried to help us figure out what was going on, but nobody had a clue.

One of the cool things about my wheelchair is that it has a seat elevator. I can push a button and the seat rises up about 18 inches. There are a number of reasons for this feature. The primary reason is that it allows me to look people in the eye in a social setting. Instead of always being lower than everyone, I can raise the chair up to put myself closer to eye level. A second benefit is that it allows me to make all of my transfers downhill. For example, when I am getting into bed I can raise the chair level to be above the level of the mattress. That way it is transferring down from my seat into bed. When I am getting out of bed, the seat is lowered so that it is a down transfer again.

In this particular situation, the seat elevator came into play. I was able to raise the chair up so they could poke and prod underneath. They were wiggling wires here, pulling on things there and before I knew it, I looked over and the lights on my wheelchair were on. I wasn't sure why the lights were back on, but figured they must have fixed the problem.

The van driver and his assistant got our luggage and we were off to board our boat. An elevator took us to the boarding level. The elevator doors opened, we headed to the boarding ramp, and my heart sank. In the middle of the ramp leading down to the dock were two steps. Apparently, even though the boat was accessible, the ramp to get on the boat was not. The cruise director's idea was to transfer me into a manual wheelchair which the deckhands could carry over the steps. Then they would put my power wheelchair into push mode, take it to the edge of the steps, pick it up, carry it down, and transfer me back into it.

They transferred me exactly the same way as the airlines. I was very thankful that my pants situation had been addressed at the airport. The deckhands picked me up and carried me down the stairs in the manual chair. I told them where the switch was to put my power wheelchair into push mode, and that the easiest thing to do was let it almost roll down the stairs in a controlled manner. Basically, what they would do is hold onto the front of the chair and the back of the chair and let it go down one step at a time very slowly. I was feeling kind of bad for them because the wheelchair by itself weighs over 300 pounds. However, they did not complain. They simply moved the chair down the steps and transferred me back into it.

I hit the power button on my wheelchair but again no lights came on. Becky immediately burst into tears. As her new husband, I felt it was my duty to console her. I held out my arm and told her to come here and that I would give her a hug. She looked me square in the eye and very slowly and deliberately said, "Don't touch me." I immediately began to have some reservations about my marriage. We had been husband-and-wife for less than 24 hours and we were now facing a situation where I could do nothing to help her. Somehow, even if I had been able to hug her it would not have fixed anything and she did not want my help anyway. I knew that this was the woman that I loved. I knew that this was the woman that I wanted to spend the rest of my life with. I just didn't know if I was going to be able to survive the next seven days alone with her.

They finally decided to transfer me back into the manual wheelchair and see what they could do with the power chair. Becky pushed me up to our room while a maintenance man took my wheelchair down to parts unknown to work on it. When we arrived in our room our luggage was waiting for us. As Becky began to put things away, we found they had lost one of our bags. I wasn't sure if things could get any worse.

It wasn't more than a few minutes until the cruise director showed up to inform us that we would be receiving an on-board credit to compensate for the lost bag. Moments later, there was a knock on the door. It was a maintenance man with my wheelchair. The chair was now functioning properly and he had figured out how to make it work semi-permanently. Apparently, there was a slightly loose wire that required the seat to be moved up to turn the wheelchair on. If I used the seat elevator function to go up at least 2 inches, the power button would work fine. The major concern about this setup was that when my seat is elevated the speed of the wheelchair is cut to only 25%. I was having trouble imagining going everywhere at a drastically reduced rate of speed and my head was about to explode. Thankfully, we figured out that once it was turned on, I could lower the seat and the chair would continue to work. It was a problem that was most likely caused by the mishandling of the wheelchair on the airplane.

The good news was that we now had some extra spending money for the trip and a reasonably functional wheelchair. On top of that, we had established that the boat itself was accessible as long as we were on board, and the deckhands would take care of getting us on and off.

The first time they got me off the boat was a major experience. After spending a full day at sea, our first stop was at Barbados. In order to get off the boat, there were ten or twelve steps down to the dock level. We followed the same procedure as previously. I was transferred into a manual chair which they carried down the steps. They switched my power wheelchair into Push Mode and began the task of taking it down the steps. A complication was that this wheelchair had no easy places to hold on to. It was not designed to be pushed or carried, it was supposed to be self-propelled. With a lack of good hand holds, the deckhands were grabbing pieces that would move. One of the deckhands was leaning against the control box for the seat controls and could not figure out why the back of the chair was moving. Add to this the fact that the deckhands were all from Southeast Asia and did not speak English. I was trying to tell them what to do but none of them understood me.

Eventually, they were able to get the wheelchair down by a feat of physical strength. They rolled it down backwards, one step at a time. It goes without saying that the four men that accomplished this were a complete lather of sweat by the time it was done. They transferred me back into the chair and Becky and I were off to explore Barbados.

We got as far as the tourist welcoming center. Beyond that, I was completely surprised to find that there was not anything accessible about the island. The good news was that the welcome center was right by the dock. Of course, there was a taxi driver who insisted that he could take us for a tour around the island. I mentioned the fact that I couldn't walk and he said it was no big deal he would just put me into his car and give us a ride. I told him that we would pass but he insisted that we go. He wouldn't take no for an answer and followed us for a good five minutes trying to convince us. When it eventually sank in that we weren't going, he stormed off, stamping his feet.

After we had our fill of the little shops and stands around the dock area we headed back to the boat. Getting back on the boat was a repeat of the experience getting off. The only difference was that now the deckhands had to fight against gravity as they had to get my wheelchair up the stairs. Again, it was a feat of sheer brute strength.

Our next stop was even more adventurous. This time, there were only a limited number of dock spaces available in the port. Our boat had to anchor out in the harbor, and they ran a small boat as a ferry back and forth between the ship and the shore. Now, the plan was to transfer into a regular wheelchair, get transferred onto the ferry boat and go to shore. Apparently, the weight of the power chair and me together would be too much for the boat to handle. So when I arrived on the dock I had to wait for the next ferry to come and bring my power wheelchair.

The island was a little bit less developed than Barbados. Amazingly, it worked out that there was increased accessibility. A few of the stores just had dirt floors which meant there were no thresholds. The sidewalks were basically dirt paths which meant that there was not a problem with curb cutouts. I had to watch out for chickens crossing my path, but that was not the worst problem in the world. It was great to just get out and feel like a tourist.

The trip back to the boat was okay. On the way to the shore I was a little concerned about my personal safety. I was sitting in the manual wheelchair on the edge of the boat going through the Caribbean. There are a lot of phobias out there. I understand people have a fear of heights, a fear of closed in spaces, or a fear of spiders. I don't have any of these; what I do have is a fear of edges. When I'm in my chair, I am worried about going too close to the edge of the sidewalk and tipping over. I like to think of it as a healthy respect for edges. I always give the edges a wide berth so I'm not ever in danger. Now, on the boat I didn't have a choice about where I was sitting. There was a railing around the outside of the boat, but I was still sitting on a platform in a wheelchair that I could not control, right on the very edge. By the return trip, I was feeling a little bit more rational and took the time to look at what was actually in the water. The water was crystal clear and I could see straight to the bottom. I could see the sand, I could see the fish, I could see everything. Okay, maybe I was still a bit nervous, but at least I was able to take in the beauty of what was surrounding me.

Our third stop was in Martinique. This was actually our biggest adventure of all. This time, instead of there being just 10 or 12 steps, there were at least 25 or 30. The good news was that the previous stops had given the deckhands an opportunity to practice what they were doing. Practice aside, I was still worried that my power chair was going to get away from them as they brought it down. It is really heavy and if it got going, there was nothing they could do to stop it.

Thankfully, they got the chair down safely but by the time it was down all the rest of the people from the cruise had left for the tourist area. Becky and I were on our own. Unfortunately, the tourist area was not close by as it had been in Barbados. We didn't know how far it was, but we set off ready for anything.

Martinique was more like Barbados in the way that it was set up. There were actual sidewalks, and everything was a little bit more developed. I'm not saying that the sidewalks were in great condition, but they were there and provided somewhere safe to travel without being in the middle of traffic. At the docks, there was a low spot in the curb where I was able just to ride up onto the sidewalk. It sure looked like a curb cut to me so I was very happy about accessibility. We followed the sidewalk towards where we thought the tourist area was. After about a quarter mile, we came to a crossroad and there was no curb cut. As a matter of fact, the curb was about 12 or 14 inches high. If it had been lower, I might have considered trying to jump it, but at that height there was no way.

We looked around and found a piece of board that we were going to try to use as a ramp but it was not wide enough or long enough. The only solution was to backtrack. I went back about halfway to the dock before I found a place where the curb was low enough for me to get off the sidewalk and on to the road. Now, I was on the street and had to move quickly so that I did not run into traffic. There was enough of a break that I was able to get back to where Becky was without facing more than a car or two.

As Becky and I continued, she asked me if I knew where I was going. I told her that I wasn't really sure. It was at this moment that an angel showed up. Well, he might not have been an angel but he was the closest thing I've ever seen. He never said anything at all. I don't know if it was because he didn't speak English or because he couldn't talk. He simply looked at me, looked at Becky and motioned to follow him.

I took a deep breath, said a quick prayer and we followed. He led us down a little path that brought us out into a park. There, in the park, was a craft show and on the opposite side of the street were all of the tourist shops. The path was a little bit bumpy so I was being careful to watch where I was going and by the time that I looked up to tell him, "Thank you" he was gone.

We looked through the craft displays before setting off for the shops. Again the issue was that there were no curb cuts. I looked around the edge of the park and found a spot where the grass came right down to the roadside. It was only about half a block up from where we needed to be.

I went up to the area and waited for traffic to clear. The traffic light up at the end of the block turned red and I made my move. As I was coming down the road Becky was standing at the far corner of the park waving her hands up and down. I thought she was trying to tell me I needed to speed up because traffic was coming behind me. The wheelchair was already on high-speed and I was pushing the joystick as far as I could. Then, all of the sudden, my wheelchair stopped and did a complete U-turn right in the middle of the street. It was at this exact moment that the light at the end of the street turned green. Now, I was sitting facing traffic, unsure why my wheelchair had stopped. I don't know if the people in Martinique had never seen a person in a wheelchair before or if their traffic was just usually insane, but it sure looked like I was going to get run over.

I turned my chair around and started back down the road. In the meantime, Becky had run up to where I was stopped. She hollered to me to lift up my feet. Apparently, what she had been trying to tell me with her hand signals was that one of my feet was hanging off of the foot rest and I needed to tilt the seat of my wheelchair to lift my feet up. In the meantime, the problem with my wheelchair was that I had actually run over my own foot. My right foot was hanging down far enough that it got caught underneath the wheel, got wedged and stopped the wheelchair. She grabbed my shoe and put my foot on the footrest as I elevated my feet. We went as fast as we could to get to the corner and get off the road. Traffic was buzzing all around me: cars, motorcycles, trucks and buses. It is only a miracle that I did not get hit. Of course, we did have to take a picture of my shoe with the tread marks, just for posterity. It's kind of ironic; my shoes get very little wear. I don't walk on them, I don't scuff them, so they're usually in pretty good shape. In this instance, I had ruined a pair of shoes by having tire marks running up one side and then across the toes.

When my heart finally stopped racing, we poked around through the shops doing some "window shopping". With everything that had been going on, we needed some type of good old American-style connection. As we rounded the corner it popped right out to us. There was McDonald's. I'm not sure exactly why we wanted to eat at McDonald's, but it just felt right. The prices were out of line, the food was nowhere near as good as what we were eating on the ship and everybody there was speaking in French, but it still felt a little bit like home. Somehow, a restaurant that I usually avoid provided that "down home" feeling—go figure!

By the end of the trip, Becky and I were back on speaking terms. I was allowed to hug her again. Facing all of the elements of the strange world as just a couple had presented some challenges. The fact that we overcame these challenges together and that we had a really fun time was a great foundation for our marriage. We knew we could face obstacles and work together to overcome them while laughing, loving each other, and loving life.

Chapter Ten
What About Kids?

Becky and I had been married for a few years when we started to talk about having children. It was a major decision for us. How would my disability impact our kids? Would I be able to hold the kids? Would I be able to offer any assistance at all in taking care of them? I wouldn't be able to change diapers, what if they fell off my lap when they wiggled? How would the stress of taking care of children add to Becky's workload, as she was already taking care of me? These were questions that the two of us had to face together. Sitting down, we talked about them, we prayed about them and we talked about them some more.

In addition to these, I was grappling with my own questions. I had concerns about kids. There were many things that I was not going to be able to do with my children. I was not going to be able to throw a football in the backyard, I was not going to be able to build a tree house, I was not going to be able to hold on to the back of their bikes when they learned how to ride.

Becky listened to my concerns and as we talked together she helped me work out what a dad really is. In real life terms, a dad is someone who teaches his kids right and wrong. A dad is someone who loves his kids every day regardless of what kind of mood he is in and regardless of what they have done. A dad is the rock that you turn to when your emotions are damaged or when you skin your knee. A dad is someone who teaches you what life is truly all about.

With that understanding, it was a whole new ballgame. I could do those things. Physical limitations aside, I would be able to love a child with my whole heart. Teaching right and wrong does not require someone that can walk or throw a ball. The true meaning of life is not encapsulated in physical ability, it is instead wrapped up in the people whose lives you touch. Life is not measured by how far you can throw a football, it is measured by how deeply you love.

Trying to become pregnant puts a lot of pressure on you. That pressure turns physical intimacy into more of a science project! Our expectations, hopes, and prayers saw no results. The emotional ups and downs, the disappointments had no explanation. Both of us questioned why this was happening. Why wouldn't this work? We both love children! We love each other. We love the Lord, why wouldn't He help us?

It was frustrating to see people around us who didn't really want to have children having kids. Sometimes even seeing the kids on the Sunday School bus was difficult. Many of these kids were born to single moms. Some of them weren't being raised by their parents. All were coming from impoverished backgrounds, and it seemed like the only people that loved them unconditionally were their Sunday School teachers. We were married, we were responsible, we would love a child unconditionally, we would raise the child ourselves, what was wrong?

After months of frustration, it became obvious that we were going to have to resort to some type of medical intervention. Our first visit to the doctor to talk about in vitro fertilization was very uncomfortable. Becky and I sat in the waiting room, looking at each other, waiting to see the nurse. Neither one of us said much as we sat there. Finally, we met with Margie. She gave us all kinds of statistics about what we could expect.

It was really difficult to get our minds around exactly what she was saying. She was throwing numbers around about the possibilities and percentages of people that use in vitro fertilization that have twins, triplets, quadruplets and more. She was saying the numbers, but what I heard was that there was a possibility we could get pregnant. That was what we wanted, that was what we'd been praying for. If this was what it took for us to get pregnant, then full speed ahead. Regardless of the percentages, regardless of the numbers, this was what we needed to do.

Becky started on the regime of pills and injections. My heart bled for her as I watched her get stuck like a pincushion on a fairly regular basis. It seemed like every time I turned around she was getting a shot of something. The shots went on for a few months until finally it was time for the procedure. I was so excited about it and so was she. This was going to be the answer to our prayers and we knew it.

Becky was chomping at the bit to do her first pregnancy test. She waited an appropriate amount of time, took the test and was devastated with the results. We were not pregnant. Someone reminded us that sometimes the pregnancy tests don't pick up on it right away so maybe we should be patient and it would happen. It only took a few days for her period to start and confirm what the pregnancy tests had said, we were not pregnant.

It felt like we had been let down. We had prayed about this, we felt like we were doing what we were supposed to, and yet it had not worked. This wasn't something that we had just done on a whim, we truly felt like this was what God had led us to do. Now, it hadn't worked. Months of shots, entirely too many weeks of waiting, countless hours of praying, and it just hadn't worked. It was frustrating and depressing all at the same time.

Becky and I were both fighting with our own emotions. Becky was struggling with the fact that she had just gone through all of this work, all of these shots, all of the medication for nothing. She wanted to be a mom, she was doing everything possible to make it happen, and now it just wasn't working. She had done everything that she could and it just didn't matter. I was feeling very inadequate and helpless as I realized that this whole experience was basically because of me. Additionally, there was nothing that I could do to comfort Becky. She didn't want to be consoled, she wanted to be pregnant, and nothing that I could do would make her the mother that she wanted to be.

Becky was an amazing trooper through this whole thing. She was immediately ready to start another round of in vitro. I wasn't so certain about this. We prayed about it, looking for peace. Becky was much more settled that we should go through another round than I was. Again, I was plagued with questions. Was this the Lord trying to tell us that we shouldn't do this? What would happen to Becky if the second round failed? That one in particular was weighing heavily on me. Insurance was only going to pay for two rounds, then what were we going to do? As difficult as the letdown was from the first go-round, how would Becky handle the stress and frustration of another failure? She was so settled. Did she have true peace from God or just a personal determination that it had to work?

Becky had her peace, but it took me a little longer to come to the same understanding. After a few weeks of prayer, I began to understand that regardless of what would happen, the Lord would be with us. If it didn't work, He would be there, if it did work, we would need Him more than ever! With that understanding, we decided to move ahead with the second round.

The failure of the first round made me much more aware of all that was actually involved in what we were doing. I began to actually dread the times that Becky would be taking her shots. I watched as she would take one in the morning and another at night. No longer were the shots just painful to her, it was pain that I felt inside as well. The uncertainty of not knowing what was going to happen made it even worse. Was this really the right thing to do? Was I involved in setting my wife up for a major disappointment as well as the pain that she was enduring with each passing shot?

Somehow, it seemed like we were getting the whole family involved in the process. Because I couldn't give her the shots and she couldn't administer them to herself, her sister Barb had to do it. Little did the family realize just how involved they would be in the upcoming years.

There was not a whole lot I could do for Becky besides be there, and pray for her. My goal was to be with her at any time that my presence would be a comfort. When it came time to actually do the implantation, it was my privilege to drive her to the hospital and hold her hand during the process. The nurse told us that she would be implanting four little embryos. She said that they had all begun to develop into at least four cells and that we had a pretty good chance of one of them working. Part of me was overjoyed, yet the cynical part of me realized that it was this nurse's job to promote optimism. There was no way that she was going to tell us that this was not going to work. She could not believe that and still find purpose in her work.

Becky was wheeled down the hall to a surgical suite. I followed behind her in my wheelchair. The process didn't take long at all and we were on our way home in 45 minutes. It all went so fast. There seemed to be an enormous amount of optimism from the nursing staff and now all we could do was pray and wait.

Patience and anticipation don't easily coexist! Becky and I were both on pins and needles waiting for the first opportunity to do a pregnancy test. We waited the recommended number of days and tested. The results of the test were inconclusive! There were supposed to be two lines and there was one dark line and one light line. We had to wait a couple of days and test again. This time the results were a little more conclusive, there was one dark line and one kind of dark line. That was enough for us! We were overjoyed with the understanding that we were pregnant!

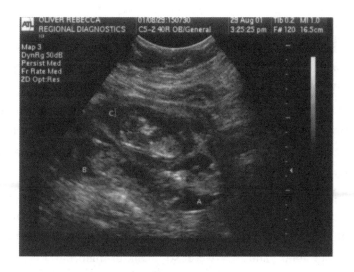

Chapter Eleven
No More Sonograms

Things moved very quickly after that! It was just a few weeks later that Becky's mother took her for her first sonogram. I told her to be sure and call me at work to let me know the details of the ultrasound. As you can imagine, I had a hard time working as I waited for her phone call. When it did come, Becky told me, "Guess what? They think they found two of them!" Sure enough, when I got home from work that day, there on the refrigerator was a little black-and-white grainy printout. It showed a black background with two little white dots on it. A whole new wave of emotions ran over me! This was fantastic! Not only did it document the fact that we were pregnant, but we were going to have twins!

I had all kinds of questions. Do we know if they're identical? Are we sure that both of them are okay? Is this going to create extra risk for Becky? The answers came back fairly quickly. No, they are not identical. Each was in its own sack. As far as the babies being okay, it was way too early to know anything about them. Finally, about extra risk for Becky, her obstetrician, Dr. Selednik, had been involved in the births of many multiples, twins, triplets, quadruplets and more. That took a lot of weight off my shoulders, knowing that he knew what he was doing and would take great care of her.

My mind started racing about twins. If they're not identical, that meant that we could have one of each. That would be so neat, a boy and a girl all in one shot. This was what we had been praying about and we were so thankful that the Lord had answered our prayers. My father-in-law even said that he had hoped that one of his children would have twins. All this excitement had me greatly anticipating the next sonogram. What would it say about our new babies? How would they be growing? What would their development look like?

Three weeks later Becky went for that next sonogram. This sonogram took a lot longer than the other one had. It took a lot longer for Becky to call me and tell me what was happening. I wasn't sure what this meant, but I was hoping that it didn't mean something bad. Imagine my surprise when the phone call came and Becky said, "Honey, they think they heard a third heartbeat!" A third heartbeat, wait . . . that meant a third baby! We weren't having twins, we were having triplets! My immediate reaction was to tell Becky, "No more sonograms!"

Arriving home from work I was greeted with yet another grainy black-and-white picture. It showed two distinct white dots and a kind of gray area in the background that was marked with a letter "C". It was at this point that the letters A, B and C took on a whole new meaning. Each of those tiny white dots was now assigned a letter. It was based on where they were positioned and that letter was going to stick with them for the duration of the pregnancy. I wasn't sure how they were going to keep track of which letter went with which baby, but they told me that the embryos were not going to move.

The concept of triplets opened up a whole new minefield of questions. Now that there were three of them, did this pose a risk to Becky? Did it make it more risky for each of them? And by the way, how did this happen? The doctor's office made it very clear that this pregnancy was high risk. Becky's age and personal health were definitely in her favor. Still, they were going to have to monitor her on a regular basis to make sure that everybody was doing okay, Mommy and all three babies.

The next question that popped into my mind was about their genders. Did we know their genders? Were they all the same? When we were thinking that they were just twins, I was hoping for one of each. Now I realized that we would likely have one of each, and I would just take number three as an added bonus regardless of gender.

Initially, we started with sonograms every two weeks. I wasn't able to take off work for every sonogram, but being at a few of them was truly a highlight. It seemed like we were able to track their development from sonogram to sonogram. We were able to see arms and legs, then a profile, then feet and hands. It didn't take too long before we were asking about their genders. While there was a little bit of uncertainty at the beginning, we soon found out that we were expecting two girls and a boy.

The whole pregnancy thing was new to me. Becky had been around her sister Barb when she was pregnant and knew a little bit, but I had never had any experience. Again, there was not a whole lot that I felt I could do for Becky. The only thing that I could think of was to give her a back rub as often as she would ask. I know that you cannot become increasingly pregnant, but the fact is that she was becoming more and more pregnant. The more pregnant she got, the more back rubs she needed and the more I was willing to give them.

I was really amazed at how Becky progressed through the whole pregnancy. She did not have a tremendous amount of problems with morning sickness. For many years I had thought that she was the most beautiful thing that God had ever created. Now that she was pregnant, she was radiantly beautiful. In addition to that, I was amazed that from behind you could hardly tell that she was pregnant, even in the later stages.

It didn't take too long before the sonograms moved from being every two weeks to weekly. Additionally, they began to do monitoring for Becky and for the babies. She would go in and they would hook up some wires to her belly and listen to the three separate heartbeats. She would come home with a little paper that had squiggly lines on it representing the heartbeat of each of our three babies. Being an absolute neophyte, I was enamored with everything "baby" and even just the concept of looking at a paper printout of the baby's heartbeat was exciting to me.

The excitement about the whole experience was overwhelming for everybody. Becky's mom became a regular fixture at our house, helping us in every way that she could. She was helping with cooking, helping with keeping Becky healthy,

94

helping with laundry and cleaning, and generally just wearing herself out. Becky decided it was time for her mom to have a break. After checking with the doctor about her own condition and the condition of the children, she felt comfortable telling her mom to take a few days to go to Florida and relax. While her mom wasn't sure about the whole situation, she agreed because she was absolutely exhausted. The day she left Becky was scheduled to go in for a monitoring. At that monitoring, the doctor decided that Becky was beginning to show signs of toxemia. These monitorings were an outpatient procedure, so we were expecting her to come home. Dr. Selednik told Becky that they were keeping her in the hospital.

Becky told Dr. Selednik that she didn't think that was going to work. She was doing a very good job at bedrest by being at home. Dr. Selednik told her that they were going to schedule the delivery by cesarean section for the next day. Becky told him that he couldn't do that, because her mom wasn't there. She informed him that her mother had just gone to Florida to recuperate from helping her so much and that she could not have the babies without her mom. Dr. Selednik informed her that this was not a negotiable situation, that her health demanded that the babies be delivered quickly.

Assessing the situation from a medical standpoint, at 34 weeks the babies were at a crucial point in their development. Because they were going to be delivered early, they needed some steroids to enhance lung development. The more time between the administration of the steroids and the delivery the better. Becky was finally able to prevail upon Dr. Selednik for an extra day before delivery. She called her mom to let her know what was going on and tell her that she needed to get back as quickly as possible. I called my mom and dad as well to let them know what was happening.

Everything had been rolling along smoothly up to this point, now things seem to be happening in fast-forward. It was true that we knew that the babies were coming, but they were coming "eventually". Now we were face-to-face with the fact that the doctor was telling us that the babies were coming in two days! When I arrived at the hospital to see Becky, she was lying in bed. She looked a little pale, but apart from that she still looked healthy and beautiful! She was smiling as she told me about her back-and-forth banter with the doctor about when the babies would be delivered. Part of me was glad to see that she was feeling well enough to inform everybody of exactly what she wanted. Another part of me worried that she would push things too far and there would be complications.

With all the tests and monitoring that were going on we didn't have much time to talk. Things were crazy and moving rapidly. It seemed like we went from the monitoring to the delivery room in a single step. The blur of action blended the day and a half from the monitoring to the delivery into a single stream of fluid motion. It seemed like every time I blinked there was something new going on, but before I had the chance to absorb it something else was going on. There was a steady flow of family members coming in and out of Becky's room. Part of this was a blessing, because there is no one that you would rather have with you during difficult circumstances than your family and the people you love. Another part of that was simply more commotion and added turmoil to the already tumultuous situation.

The next day was Wednesday. I went to work for part of the day because they told me that the babies would not be delivered until Thursday. I'm fairly certain that I did not get anything accomplished at all. My body may have been at work, but my mind and my heart were in Becky's hospital room. As soon as I had put in a few hours, I was racing back to the hospital to be with her. When I came in, Becky was not in her room but was gone for tests. One of the nurses at the nursing station offered me a quick tour of the neonatal intensive care unit. She hoped to familiarize me with the part of the hospital where the babies would be. Looking in the window I was able to see four trays with warming lamps over them. The nurse explained that the children would need help in regulating their body temperature once they were born and the lamps would help keep them warm. I was introduced to the staff on duty. There was one other child in the unit and the staff was very attentive. I asked how they would handle a sudden influx of three children. They had planned to have a slight increase in staffing to make sure that all of the children in the unit were receiving the necessary care and were handled with the highest priority. After the tour, it was back to the room, more family member visits, another test, and then I went back home.

I was bursting with excitement as I drove to the hospital the following morning. This was going to be the big day! The moment that we had been anticipating for the last seven and a half months had finally arrived. The more I thought about it, it wasn't just the anticipation of the last seven and a half months, it was the culmination of the past few years of hoping, praying and waiting. When I arrived, there was a new bustle of activity. Sherrie McGown, a friend of ours, worked at the hospital. She was so excited about the babies coming that she was in touch with the public relations department and was setting up a press release about their impending arrival.

I wasn't sure why they were going to make a press release for our children. With all of the medical intervention that was involved in fertility these days, a set of triplets being born was not necessarily newsworthy. As I talked to the public relations director, he explained that the circumstances around the arrival of our babies were exceptional. Having triplets was one facet, use of in vitro fertilization was another, a quadriplegic father was another facet, and the story of love between two people in the midst of difficult circumstances was another facet. Together, these all made for a gem of a story. I smiled as I realized that I wasn't the only one that had a bad sense of humor.

Finally it was time for the delivery. By the time I was finished with the public relations people Becky had been moved down to the delivery area. We already knew the delivery was going to be by caesarean section, so she was in one of the labor rooms waiting for the delivery team to be assembled. I arrived in the room just in time for a few quick pictures and some videotaping of a last comment. Becky's mom had still not arrived, but now we knew that she was on a flight home and would be arriving soon. My parents had not arrived either, but they were on their way.

A nurse appeared to inform us that it was time for the delivery. All of the family members had to stay out of the delivery room, the only person that was allowed in besides Becky was me. As they prepared Becky for the delivery, they erected a huge sheet that covered our view of the operating area. Amazingly enough, this was the first time that we'd had a chance to talk as a couple since the delivery had been scheduled. I took a moment to tell her how excited I was, that I love her very much and that I was so happy that she was the mother of my children. The only part of her that wasn't covered was her face and all I could do was reach out to brush her cheek and tell her that I knew that she was going to be a great mom.

Since I was the only one allowed in the delivery room, the family had entrusted me with the video camera. As soon as I realized that things were about to happen, I turned it on and started recording. I was pretty sure that I was doing a great job, but in retrospect it didn't quite turn out like I had hoped. With my hands as limited as they are, I wasn't able to hold the camera at a real good angle. When we finally had a chance to watch the tape, we had to tilt our heads to the side to make sure that we could see the picture straight.

Dr. Selednik said something like, "Here we go." As I turned the camera towards the sheet, Becky and I came to a startling realization. We had been talking about names, but we weren't settled on which ones we were going to use. We knew that we had a baby A, baby B, and baby C, that there were two girls and a boy, but we still did not have all three names set in stone. No sooner had we made that realization than I heard a tiny cry. The first baby delivered was baby C, a boy. Fortunately, we were both settled on the boy's name. Quickly, a nurse held him up over the top of the sheet. They asked what his name was and I said, "Joshua." A minute later, baby B followed, a little girl. Again, we were pretty settled about this one and when they held her up I told them that her name was Lauren. Now we were at a critical juncture because we did not have a consensus on the third name. We only had a minute to wait before baby A was delivered. We had a quick look at baby A over the top of the sheet. I looked at Becky, she looked at me and we both said, "Chloe";

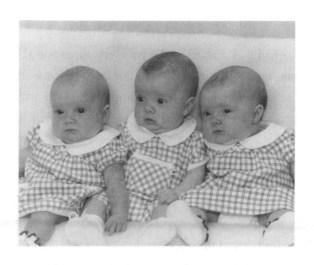

Chapter Twelve
Daddy!

As each baby was born, they were whisked from the delivery room to the neonatal intensive care unit. The fact that they were six weeks premature created no small problems. I didn't realize at the time what a blessing it was to hear each of the children cry as they were being born. Each cry meant that we had a breathing and functioning baby. It did not take too long before the word came back that the children were having some trouble breathing. They were not absorbing oxygen as quickly as they should and they needed some specialized care. The fact that all three of them needed this meant it was too overwhelming for the hospital where we were. They were going to have to transfer them to the Western Pennsylvania Hospital in downtown Pittsburgh.

Becky had just arrived in the recovery room and the family was beginning to be allowed in to see her. It was an intense mixture of joy and concern at the same time. The triplets had finally arrived! They all looked relatively healthy, but there was this issue with their breathing. Because the babies had been delivered by cesarean section there was no way that Becky was able to be transferred at the same time. Additionally, the ambulance could only carry a single isolette at a time and there was only room for 2 babies per isolette so they were going to have to be transferred in two separate ambulances.

We had a steady stream of doctors coming through to check on Becky. With each one the first question was how the children were doing. It seemed like we were not getting very many updates. In the meantime, my cell phone rang and it was a reporter from the newspaper. He had received word that the children had been born and now it was time for us to do a quick interview. I'm not sure how I managed to answer any of his questions or concentrate on what was going on as the room was a bustle of activity. Becky's bed was on one side of the room and there were family members all around her, doctors and nurses were entering and exiting the room on a regular basis and everyone was talking at once. I wheeled over to a corner of the room and proceeded to do our interview there.

Almost as soon as I was done the interview, they began to bring the children in so that we could see them before they were transferred. Each of them was assigned a transfer nurse. The nurse would wheel the isolette into the room, tell us which baby it was, give us a quick peek into the isolette and then they were off to the ambulance. As this was happening, we decided that Mary Ellen (the wife of Becky's brother Tom) and I would go down to West Penn. Becky was going to be kept in Forbes Regional Hospital until she recovered enough to transfer. I gave her a quick kiss, told her that I loved her and was on my way.

I don't remember any of the trip to West Penn. I'm not sure how I got there, I'm not sure how long it took, I just know that I could not wait to get there. When I arrived at the neonatal intensive care unit things were really moving quickly. The unit was divided into six pods. Each of those pods had room for six babies. In order to properly do the intake and assessment on each of the children, they were each sent to a different pod. I felt a little bit like a lost puppy as I wandered from pod to pod looking at my children. Lauren and Josh were breathing adequately by just increasing the oxygen mixture in their isolettes. Chloe, on the other hand, needed some additional oxygen and they had a little tube that ran up to her nose. It was taped to the side of her face and I could not stand it. Here was this beautiful little child and how was she going to feel when they took that tape off?

For the first two hours there was not anything that I needed to do. I spent the time wandering between the three isolettes. I was afraid to open the isolettes, so I did the only thing that I could think of. I stopped by each child and prayed with them, then told them that I loved them. When things finally calmed down, I got up the courage to ask the nurse in Chloe's pod when we might be able to hold the kids. She responded by asking me, "Would you like to hold her now?" I asked if it would be okay, or would it jeopardize her health in any way. The nurse assured me it would be fine.

As I prepared to hold my child for the first time my heart was in my throat. My hands were scrubbed and I was dressed in a blue drape. The nurse opened the side of the isolette and carefully pulled Chloe out. I could barely contain my enthusiasm and my absolute joy. Carefully I arranged my arms to form a safe spot for her to lie. As she was gently placed in my arms I could hardly help myself as tears flowed down my face. This was truly a gift from God. This child was absolutely beautiful, her teeny nose, her cute little mouth, her tiny fingers and those eyes that batted open every now and then to look up at me. Quietly in the background, there was a radio playing and it just so happened that these words sang out across the room, "You are so beautiful to me." I couldn't think of any more appropriate words to describe the feelings inside.

The little child I was holding in my arms represented so much potential. Looking down at her I couldn't help but think about the life that I would enjoy with her. It only took a few seconds to imagine the progress she would make. She would come home from the hospital, grow, take her first steps, head off to her first day of school, graduate, go off to college, get a job, get married, and move out of my house. Almost immediately I was feeling the loneliness of her leaving the house before my mind was brought back to reality as I looked at her face. She was only a baby. She was only hours old and we were going to have a long time together. I promised her that no matter how big she got, no matter how old she was and no matter where she was, I would always be her daddy and I would always love her.

I was feeling the internal struggle of a new parent. Part of me wanted to hold her forever and another part of me wanted her to get back into the isolette as quickly as possible so that I did not break her. After a few minutes, the nurse said it was time to put her back. As the nurse took her and placed her back in the isolette I thought to myself that these three children tied with my wife for being the most beautiful things that God created. By this time it was late and I really needed to get home. I made one last round and told all three of them that Daddy loved them very much and I would be back tomorrow.

With my heart overflowing with love and happiness, I got in the van to drive home. The entire world had something of a new appearance to me. I wondered if every new parent had as much happiness as I. Driving home, I thought about just how wonderful it would be to raise these kids. I was their dad, and I had the responsibility to protect these tiny lives from everything that was bad.

As I drove, everything was larger than life. I was much more aware of my surroundings. I noticed the traffic lights, the street signs, the people, the storefront windows and just about anything else that was there. One of these people stood out to me.

I first noticed her from a distance. She had long blond hair that flowed down her back. She was wearing high heels, a short skirt and a brightly colored jacket. Her outfit was definitely designed to draw attention to herself. As I got closer to her, my perception changed drastically. My first impression had been that this was a younger woman, but I realized that she was a little bit older than I had originally thought. The long blond hair that was so attractive from a distance was not so beautiful close-up. It was definitely not her original color as dark roots were evident.

I quickly realized that even though her entire outfit was designed to draw attention to her "physical attributes", she was not what she appeared to be. My mind immediately started to run. Here was a woman that was trying to attract attention by emphasizing her physical appearance. It seemed so sad that even though her outward appearance was not what it once was, she felt that it was all she had.

I immediately began to wonder if anyone looked at this woman the way that I looked at my little girls. It was an assumption on my part, but I was fairly certain that nobody was as concerned about her well-being as I was about my little girls' well-being. I thought about my little girls as they would grow up. I remembered the rapid timeline that had run through my mind: walking, going to school, graduating, and getting married. I determined immediately that the boys that were going to be coming to my house, wanting to date my daughters, all had to pass a simple test. If they weren't as interested in my girls' well-being as I was, then get out of my house.

Chapter Thirteen
Little Feet

I was having a great time visiting the kids in the hospital. It seemed like they were making progress every day. Lauren and Josh were soon able to breathe room air without any oxygen added to it. Chloe progressed from having an oxygen tube to just having the air in her isolette enriched with oxygen, then she too was able to breathe room air. They were feeding from bottles and it was a delight to be a part of that process.

The general wisdom is that children delivered prematurely will be in the hospital until their due date. Our kids were making good progress and after only a week and a half the doctor brought up the subject of them going home. We were delighted with the prospect, running back and forth to the hospital wasn't that much fun. The fact that they were "getting out early" meant that they were doing well. In the midst of all these positive signs, I think we completely overlooked the fact that we were bringing three babies home. It was time to put all of the parenting talk into action. All the things a dad is supposed to do were going to need done. This was where the rubber met the road, the babies were coming home.

Lauren and Josh went in Becky's car with her and Barb. Becky's mom and Chloe rode in my van. I don't believe that I have ever driven quite so carefully in my entire life as the first time I had such precious cargo in my vehicle. The speed limit became a mandate instead of a suggestion. I stopped at yellow lights, always used my turn signal and kept a safe cushion between me and the car in front of me (actually, it was more like twice as much space as what is recommended.)

It didn't take long to assess what I could actually do with the babies. I could hold them on my lap, I could feed them a bottle, I could talk to them and sing to them. The list of what I couldn't do was a lot longer. I couldn't change diapers (although, I admit that it wasn't something that I was absolutely dying to do,) I could not lift the kids in and out of their cribs, I couldn't really bathe the kids, and burping them just didn't seem to work for me somehow.

I will say this about my wife: Becky is the queen of organization. She likes to have a plan for everything. In this particular case, she looked at what needed to be done, looked at what I could do and we worked out a plan together. I think the best example of this is the middle of the night feeding. In some ways, it seems like one of those three cups and a ball tricks.

108

You're going to need to follow along closely as they need fed, burped (twice) and changed.

All three kids were sleeping together in a Pack-and-Play in our room. We would not wake them; it was a matter of them waking up when they were hungry. Now, once the first one was awake (usually Chloe) everyone would get what they needed.

When Chloe woke up, Becky would change her diaper and give her to me so I could feed her and Becky would burp her. By that time, Lauren would stir and Becky would get her up and change her while I gave Chloe her second feeding. It was then time for Chloe to be burped again and I would get Lauren to feed. I gave Lauren her first feeding while Becky burped Chloe and put her back in bed. She would then get Josh up and change him. I would get Josh for his first feeding while Becky would burp Lauren. Then she would burp Josh while I fed Lauren the rest of her bottle. We would switch and I would get Josh for the second time while she burped Lauren and put her back to bed. Finally, she would burp Josh for the second time and put him back in bed. After some practice, we got the process down to about 45 minutes. It was a pretty efficient system! In 45 minutes we were able to get three babies up, change their diapers, feed them a full bottle and burp each one twice. Of course, the process was repeated at 11 p.m., 3 a.m. and 7 a.m.

I'm not sure how either of us survived. The 11 p.m. feeding meant that we never got to sleep before midnight. The 3 a.m. feeding meant that we got our sleep in three hour chunks at best. The 7 a.m. feeding meant that we were getting up at our normal time. Somehow, in the middle of all that, I was still working full time and Becky was taking care of three babies while I was at work.

Having Becky's family in the area was a huge help. Becky's mom was at the house almost every day. Barb and her husband, Mike, lived next door and so they were over on a regular basis as well. Our house became a model for the division of labor. The babies needed to be fed, changed and bathed. The rest of the family needed to be fed. The house needed to be cleaned and the laundry needed done (among all the rest of the regular household chores.) You could have mistaken our home for a military operation as everybody seemed to have "marching orders". The bustle of activity would die down for a few moments while everyone ate dinner, but then it would pick right back up as the kids would need their baths, they would need to be dressed and then fed, the table needed cleaned, the dishes needed washed and who knows what else. Everyone was given a job.

One evening, I found out that I had a skill that no one else had. I was holding Lauren on my lap while she was crying and fussing. It didn't seem like anything would calm her down. I tried singing, I tried talking, and nothing worked. I drove from the kitchen to the living room and while I was driving, the crying and fussing slowed down. When I stopped, it picked back up. Needless to say, it only took a few seconds before I realized what was going on. For years, people have said that the easiest way to get a baby to sleep is to go for a ride in the car. I had my own vehicle right in the house. When the kids were fussy, I could drive them around in my wheelchair and they would calm down. When they were having difficulty going to sleep, I would drive in circles with them on my lap and it didn't take too awful long before they were sound asleep.

The impact of this discovery was huge. First, I could contribute in a way that no one else could. Second, it allowed for some great bonding time with the kids. Third, it was a way in which my situation was actually an asset. Fourth, it showed me that even though my situation was different, it would allow for some unique opportunities in my relationship with my children.

Progress happens very quickly with infants. It didn't take very long at all before they were eating baby food and crawling around. These were no small accomplishments, since it meant that I could now get them out of their cribs because they could crawl to me. Additionally, eating baby food meant a whole new set up for mealtime.

The problem was how to feed three children at one time. They were all hungry, but feeding them individually was either time-consuming or required three people. Becky's resourcefulness kicked into high gear. She lined their highchairs up side-by-side at the back of the kitchen. She would prepare enough food for all of them and then sit in a wheeled office chair. She simply rolled across the line, giving each of them a bite, then rolled back. It was sheer genius. My only contention was that the child in the middle always got twice as much because she was fed going and coming.

Once the kids could crawl, it didn't take very long before they were trying to stand. With the variety of hand holds on my wheelchair, it was the perfect place for them to "pull up". Of course, as a new father, everything that they did was amazing to me. The thing about them pulling up on my wheelchair was that I knew it was moving towards the day when they could pull themselves up onto my lap.

I have to say that every stage that my kids went through was my new favorite stage. The growth and progress they were showing was amazing and it seemed like each new stage brought new ways to connect.

The kids didn't get too old before I became concerned about those connections. They were receiving a lot of negative feedback. It seemed that they were constantly being told to "stop that" or "don't do that". On top of that, they were often given attention only when they were involved in negative behaviors. I decided that it would be very valuable to provide positive reinforcement. I wanted to reinforce the value of doing good things.

The system that I came up with was called "Gold Stars". I printed gold stars onto index cards and created a board to put the stars on. I told them that I would award them gold stars when they went "above and beyond". This was not just a way to reinforce them doing what they were supposed to, it was to encourage them to look for opportunities to do something good. Whenever I saw something that I approved of, I would award them a gold star and they could put it up on the board underneath their name.

Once they had collected five gold stars, they were able to trade them in for something special. It might be a prize from the store, a "date" with Mom or Dad, getting out of a chore or something else that they really wanted. The kids got this concept very quickly and were gung ho.

We hadn't been utilizing the gold stars for very long when we hit the first bump in the road. One morning while I was getting dressed, all three children were in our bedroom. They were talking and laughing and having a very good time. I asked Josh to do something and he ignored me. I asked him again and he ignored me again. Finally, I told him, "If you don't listen, I am going to take down one of your gold stars." Unfortunately for him, he still didn't listen.

Once I finished getting dressed, I got him on my lap and took him out to the kitchen where the gold star board hung on the wall. The two of us had a discussion about how important it was to listen to Mom and Dad the first time they said something. Since I had told him that I was going to take a gold star down if he didn't listen, I knew I had to follow through on my promise. Josh burst into tears, begging me not to take the gold star down. When I reached for the gold star board, he literally melted off my lap onto the floor into a sobbing puddle.

I started to rethink what I was doing. I had not counted on him being so attached to the gold star and so devastated by taking one away. Was I being too rough on him? Would it really hurt if I just let him go this one time? I was seriously considering telling him that I was going to let him get away with it this time, but the next time was going to be for sure.

Before I could tell him what I was thinking, the girls found out what was going on. Chloe and Lauren rushed over to where we were standing. With big tears in their eyes, they began to beg me not to take down Josh's gold star. I suddenly realized that as a parent, I had to do what I said. If I wasn't serious about the ultimatums I set out, they weren't going to mean anything to the children, ever. With a feeling of great heaviness in my heart, I told them that the gold star had to come down because Josh had not listened. The two of them started to cry harder and ran off to their cribs to get snuggled in with their blankies.

I had taped the gold star cards onto the board and with my limited finger strength, I was having a great deal of difficulty getting the card off. Things were quiet for a moment as the girls were finding comfort in their cribs and Josh had wound down to a bit of a whimper. Just as I got the card off the board, Chloe came running out of the bedroom. Instead of calming down, she was now crying harder than she had been. I picked her up on my lap and held her and asked, "Chloe, what's the matter?" She said, "Daddy, I miss you when you are in jail!"

I didn't think I understood her properly. "What did you say?" She repeated herself, "Daddy, I miss you when you're in jail." I asked her why she thought I was going to go to jail. She told me, "Lauren use her play cell phone to call the police. She tell them that you take Josh's Gold Star and they come put you in jail!"

I assured her that I was not going to jail. There were two important lessons that I learned that day. First, you have to carry through on everything you say to your children. If you tell them you are going to do something, you have to carry it out. It goes the same for promises as well as punishments. If you say you are going to be at the baseball game, you have to be at the baseball game. If you say that you are going to put them in time out if they do something, you have to put them in time out when they do it. The second lesson that I learned is that your kids will always think that they are smarter than you. It started at age 3 and it hasn't stopped since.

Chapter Fourteen
One Step at a Time

Life's pathway is a series of ups and downs. It lays before us and our level of engagement and enjoyment are affected by our focus. Things happen, life happens, it's up to us how we choose to look at it.

It was my first summer working for the Disability Rights Network of Pennsylvania. In my travels from the parking garage to my office, I went right by the County building. There was a large fountain in the courtyard and they often held special events there. A sign outside the Courtyard announced upcoming events.

The one that caught my eye was a free cookout. It was going to be held at lunchtime on a Friday. I figured a cookout sounded fun and a free lunch was a good thing. I envisioned burgers on the grill with chips and soda.

When I arrived, I was slightly disappointed. There were two or three college students standing beside a grill cooking hotdogs. I figured it wasn't a hamburger, but there's no problem with the free hotdog either. I took my hotdog and looked around to see what else there was to offer. There weren't any chips, but there was an area with condiments and a large cooler of Pepsi.

I decided that I wanted ketchup on my hot dog. The thing that I was concerned about was spilling on myself. Since I had to go back to work, I was concerned that I keep a professional appearance and not have a giant ketchup stain on my pants. In order to make that work, I asked one of the college students to help me. The young man was very nice and grabbed the ketchup bottle. He opened the top, flipped the bottle upside down and squirted a line of ketchup right down my pant leg.

He apologized and grabbed a napkin to wipe it off. I thanked him for his help, but was thinking to myself that I probably could have done that just as well myself. Feeling slightly bummed, I finished my hot dog and went off in search of a drink. It was nice and warm outside so the Pepsi cooler looked very inviting with condensation running down the side. When I got in front of it, there was a sign on the door that read, "Sorry, we are all out."

I shook my head. I thought, "You have got to be kidding me!" So much for this glorious cookout that I had envisioned in my mind. All I was getting was a hot dog and a ketchup stain. I looked at my watch and realized that since I had only had a hot dog, I still had a large chunk of my lunch break left. Since it was so warm I figured that I could salvage the day by going to 7-11 and getting a Slurpee. The great news was that there was a 7-11 just a few blocks down the way.

116

I made my way down to the 7-11 and got myself the largest cola flavored Slurpee that they had. I wedged the cup down between my legs to hold it still and headed back to my office. All the bumps in the sidewalk presented major obstacles to be avoided. I had to take each of them slowly to make sure that the Slurpee did not spill. After delicate negotiation, I managed to arrive back at the office safely and headed up the elevator to my office.

When I arrived at the floor for our office, I headed out the door of the elevator. The problem was that the elevator lurched slightly as I headed towards the door. That was a movement I had not been planning on and just like that my Slurpee flipped over onto the floor of the elevator. It's amazing just how much a large Slurpee cup can contain. Embarrassed and frustrated, I headed back down to the lobby to tell the security guard what had happened.

When the doors opened, I was further embarrassed as the female college interns from the Law offices upstairs were all getting into my elevator. It was borderline humiliation as I had to warn them to be careful because I had spilled my Slurpee. I'm not sure what they were thinking, but in my mind they were all saying, "Look at the poor guy in a wheelchair."

I told Edie, our security guard, what had happened and asked her to have maintenance clean it up. With that, I headed back to the office. I was feeling fairly demoralized. All I had for lunch was a hot dog, no chips, no soda and now, no Slurpee. When I entered the office, the look on my face must have been pretty bad. Johnetta, our administrative assistant, asked me what was wrong.

I explained to her what had happened. Her first reaction was to say that she was getting ready to go for a walk on her lunch break and that she would be delighted to stop by 7-11 and pick up a new Slurpee for me. I told her that I would be thrilled with that, and headed back to my office. Just as I headed down the hallway, my embarrassment deepened further. The fire alarm for the building went off. That wasn't such a big problem until the explanation came over the loudspeaker from Edie. She said that it was no big deal, they were just cleaning up a mess in the elevator.

On the way down the hallway, I passed the office of my coworker, Sharon. While I was slightly happier, I still must have been pretty out of sorts. She asked me what was wrong as well. I explained the whole situation to her, the miserable lunch, the spilled Slurpee and the pants stain. Sharon responded that she carried a stain stick in her purse. She pulled it out and applied it to the stain on my pants. Just that quickly, the stain was gone.

It didn't take very long before Johnetta came back with my Slurpee. Apart from the embarrassment, I was now just about back to where I started. I had eaten my free hotdog, I enjoyed my Slurpee and my pants were no longer stained.

It was at that point that I heard faint echoes of Beth Adams. I didn't do it exactly like everyone else. I didn't do it like I had before my injury. It didn't work out like I had planned, but I was living life. It was my life and it was good!

Epilogue

My room is still mostly dark. The light of dawn is beginning to brighten things up a little bit. In looking back on the experiences that I've been through, I start to realize that I'm truly blessed. The fact is that my attitude is all about what I'm focused on. My life is full of wonderful things.

I could complain about my job, but the fact is that among people with disabilities the unemployment rate is over 70%. I have a job and I should be very thankful for that. My experiences and education have put me in a position where I am able to assist other people who may not be as outspoken as I am. I may not be making millions, but I am engaged in meaningful work and I'm supporting my family.

It is true that there are things I cannot do with my children. What is going to make an impact on them is what I *am* doing with them. Spending time with them, teaching them right and wrong, establishing traditions and just loving them every day, these are the meaningful parts of life. Someday, at my funeral I want them to be able to talk about the man who loved them every day. Disability doesn't enter into that.

As far as my marriage goes, I am very fortunate. I have a woman who loves me for who I am. She can see past my physical limitations and appreciate who I am on the inside. Yes, we have our differences of opinions and what marriage doesn't? This provides us with an opportunity for us to blend our abilities together. We both have strengths and weaknesses that we bring to our relationship and to our family. Acknowledging those and being aware of them allows us to work together.

At the end of the day, everybody has problems. There are obstacles that we all face that have the potential to stop us in our tracks. The ultimate question comes down to what defines success? If we measure success in dollars and cents, the vast majority of us will only be mildly successful. If we measure success in terms of relationships, in terms of people whose lives we've touched, in terms of people that we have loved, we all have a chance at being very successful.

There are things that I can't do, there are things that you can't do. That being said, we are alive! That means that we ride on this roller coaster with its ups and downs. We get to experience the thrills and the exasperation. Instead of focusing on what we can't do, let's focus on what we can. Take hold of the things you can do. Do them with all your might. That's when life becomes full.

After remembering where I have come from, assessing where I am and looking at where I'd like to go, I'm ready for the day. Today is a gift from God, an opportunity to live life to the fullest. I'm ready to take on the day, to live, laugh, learn and love. When it comes to life's journey, I'm still walking!

Contact the author:

rob@yourmotivationalspeaker.com

(412) 450-0433

http://www.yourmotivationalspeaker.com

http://www.robsbook.com

http://www.facebook.com/imroboliver

http://www.twitter.com/imroboliver